Classroom Practices in Teaching English 1976-1977

Responses to Sexism

D1295783

Classroom Practices
in Teaching English
1976-1977

Responses to Sexism

Ouida Clapp, Chair, Committee on Classroom Practices

**Lallie Coy, Nan Harty, Ruth Lysne, Guest Editors
for Committee on the Role and Image of Women**

NCTE National Council of Teachers of English
1111 Kenyon Road, Urbana, Illinois 61801

ACKNOWLEDGMENTS: "I'm a Chicana," "Rape Report," and "The Rapist," are reprinted by permission of Rita Urias Mendoza. "X: A Fabulous Child's Story" is reprinted by permission of International Creative Management for Lois Gould. Copyright © 1972 by Lois Gould. "Thanks, Mom" is reprinted with permission from Blue Mountain Arts, Inc., from I WANT TO LAUGH, I WANT TO CRY, by Susan Polis Schutz, © 1973 by Continental Publications.

Library of Congress Cataloging in Publication Data
Main entry under title:

Responses to Sexism.

(Classroom practices in teaching English; 1975-1976)
Bibliography: p.
1. Language arts—Psychological aspects—Addresses, essays, lectures. 2. Sexism—Addresses, essays, lectures. 3. Sex role in literature—Addresses, essays, lectures. 4. Femininity (Psychology)—Addresses, essays, lectures. I. Clapp, Ouida H. II. National Council of Teachers of English. Committee on Classroom Practices. III. Series.
LB1575.8.R47   407   77-780
ISBN 0-8141-0686-2

Contents

Units on Sexism

Theory and Resources

Preface

Because Americans have found a will and a voice to demand unbiased sex-role definition, and because the members of the Committee on Classroom Practices in the Teaching of English believe that schools can and should play an important, even crucial part in removing sexism from life in America, we were pleased to agree to the suggestion of the Committee on the Role and Image of Women in the Classroom and the Profession that we use sexism as the topic for this issue of *Classroom Practices*.

At a spirited open meeting during the annual conference of the National Council of Teachers of English in San Diego, November, 1975, the Classroom Practices Committee exchanged views with participants about the focus that the topic should take, and the kind and number of articles it would attract. I am sure that the people who attended that meeting will be satisfied with what they find in this publication.

Invitations for manuscripts began to appear in the fall, 1975 issues of *Language Arts*, *English Journal*, and *College English*, as well as in newsletters and journals of many NCTE affiliates. As in past years, editors of various subject-related journals joined with us in publishing notices requesting manuscripts.

Committee on Women members Lallie Coy, Nan Harty, and Ruth Lysne served as readers who did the initial screening. They read a total of eighty-one manuscripts from twenty-six states and Vancouver, British Columbia, Canada. Assisting the editor in reading and evaluating the manuscripts submitted to the Classroom Practices Committee were members Jeffrey Golub, Norman Nathan, Sandra Seale, Gene Stanford, and Raymond Rodrigues. Manuscripts selected by the committee were read by each member of the Editorial Board.

The book is divided into four thematic sections rather than sections dealing with separate instructional levels because it is likely that all of the articles will be of interest to most readers, and the ideas and lessons are often adaptable to various levels.

That *Classroom Practices* continues to enjoy wide interest is illustrated by a recent request for the book from a principal in Wahroonga, New South Wales, Australia. The Committee appreciates such interest just as it values the comments and letters it receives from Council members and other readers across the country, and hopes that the present issue will prove to be a useful resource for teachers of English.

Introduction

Like many other social ills that become educational issues, sexism is too often relegated to study in only specific classrooms in a school, college, or university, or to only a small group of already interested and "self-selected" people. We often find its study described as "women's studies" or "women's issues." The message erroneously implied by these labels is that the study of sex roles or sex differences in language or women in literature is an area for women only. But those who study or research concerns about women know that sexism, its implications, and its ramifications affect everyone, whether consciously or unconsciously. It does influence our behavior, attitudes, and relationships—with friends, with spouses, with children, and, for the readers of this book, with students. Every time we choose a helper from the class, use Johnny or Susie as examples of behavior, grade papers, interact with individual students, select chairpersons or secretaries for class committees, tell only the girls to provide snacks for the class party, or expect the boys always to carry chairs, we may be exhibiting sexist behavior.

As teachers, our attitudes and behavior affect our students; our expectations often become theirs. If we are interested in promoting thought, individual growth, and learning in the fullest sense of the word, then we cannot condone or exhibit sexist behavior. Nor can we ignore it. Whether male or female, we are influenced by such attitudes and behavior; whether male or female, we should be aware of them as they emerge in our expectations for our students. Thus, sexism is not simply a women's issue; it is a human issue, one that involves educators, NCTE members, and students. Consequently, this book was created in the hope that it would help us combat sexism in our classrooms and in our lives.

The essential element of the articles, syllabi, and methods described in this book is their adaptability to a variety of classrooms and levels. They were not designed for special women's studies courses; rather, their formats, focuses, and specific skill objectives are those of most literature, composition, or language classes. In this year of the "basics," we have attempted to parallel the issue of sexism with basic reading, writing, and language skills for all levels. Thus, the articles can be used in almost any English classroom to help teach the communications skills most students need. Yet they have other purposes: to provide breadth through interdisciplinary study, to help bring students to awareness of their values and attitudes, to free students so that they can make viable choices, to stimulate new perceptions and thoughts. To these ends, we dedicate this issue of *Classroom Practices* to all teachers and students, both male and female.

We would like to thank the members of the Classroom Practices Committee and NCTE for encouraging our participation in this text. We also thank all those people who sent us manuscripts; it is their efforts, interest, and support that made this publication possible.

Lallie J. Coy
for the Committee on the Role and Image
of Women in the Council and the Profession

Developing Awareness

Recognizing the existence of sex-role stereotyping in books, media, and in our own minds is the first essential step in overcoming its influence. These exercises are geared mainly to elementary and middle school classes, where this recognition must begin. However, a teacher at any level who sees this need in his or her own classroom will find them easily adaptable to older groups.

Activities to Liberate Both Sexes

Gloria H. Powers
Denver, Colorado

Using concepts from the book Free to Be . . . You
and Me, *the author developed activities that helped
these elementary students see themselves and others
more clearly.*

Both boys and girls need to be liberated in their views of appropriate
roles and behavior. The following activities help to teach children to see
each person as a human being, regardless of sex. They learn to accept the
fact that stereotyped roles and behavior do not free a person, but rather
place restrictions on each sex, restrictions which hinder both boys and girls
from seeing each other as free, unique human beings.

Using the concepts expressed in the book and record *Free to Be . . . You
and Me*[1], I structured the following activities to help students see
themselves and others as whole individuals with many choices available to
them.

Activity 1

Have the students pretend they are casting parts for a play in which
certain characters are involved. The students are to give names for each
character's part. For example:

a) chemist
b) nurse
c) police officer
d) hairdresser

e) convict
f) telephone operator
g) drug addict
h) athlete

After the students have created names for each character, the teacher
should make a chart on the board with two divisions—male and female.
List the characters and place a mark under the appropriate column
whenever the students give a man's or woman's name for the role. From
this activity, the teacher can discuss stereotyped sex roles, and the reasons
why the students perceived some roles as being predominately masculine
or feminine.

---

[1] Marlo Thomas and Friends, *Free to Be . . . You and Me* (New York: McGraw-Hill
Book Company, 1974).

Activity 2

Play some selections from the record "Free to Be . . . You and Me." The record comes with a sheet of lyrics which can be duplicated easily onto transparencies for the overhead projector. Have the students follow the lyrics on the screen as they listen to the recording. After each chosen selection, discuss what the selection was trying to indicate about roles, behavior, and attitudes. One selection which is particularly good to motivate response is entitled "It's All Right to Cry."

Activity 3

Have each student create a cartoon depicting some stereotyped or traditional role or behavior expected for each sex. Have newspaper print and crayons available for the students to use. After they have finished, place each cartoon around the room so the students can see and discuss the roles and behaviors illustrated.

Activity 4

Pass out a collection of various magazines. Have the students go through the magazines and tear out advertisements which depict the sexes performing stereotyped roles. After this assignment, have the students go through the same magazine and tear out advertisements which show no stereotyping of male or female roles. This should encourage discussion of how the media affects our own perception of what is appropriate behavior for both sexes. The teacher could also use other types of media to illustrate this point.

Activity 5

Create a value sheet where students have to agree or disagree with a statement concerning behavior, attitude, and roles expected from both sexes. Included is a sampling of questions which could be placed on such a sheet. After students have completed it, allow them to explain why they agreed or disagreed with each statement.

1. It is not masculine to study to be a beautician.

        agree   disagree

2. It is not feminine to be a truck driver.

        agree   disagree

3. It is not masculine to be sensitive and kind.

        agree   disagree

4. It is not feminine to be athletic.

        agree   disagree

5. It is not masculine to cry in public.

        agree   disagree

6. It is not feminine to swear.

        agree   disagree

Activity 6

Allow the students to create their own filmstrips or slides showing some aspect of the concepts being expressed in the record "Free to Be . . . You and Me." Give them enough time to work in class on this project, and have each student or group present their filmstrips or slides to the class so they can share their responses.

Activity 7

Bring in children's picture and story books. Have the students go through the books looking for stereotyped examples of masculine and feminine characteristics and roles. The teacher could make a list of questions that the students could apply to the books being surveyed. For example, some of the questions could center around the following: (1) what type of words are used to describe the females in the story?; (2) what type of words are used to describe the males in the story?; (3) what type of jobs do the women have in the story?; (4) what type of jobs do the men have in the story?; and (5) who are the most active characters in the stories, the boys or the girls? This surveying of children's books should help older children see how at an early age they are taught what roles, behavior, and characteristics are expected from them.

As a follow-up activity, the students could create their own story or picture books where the sexes are portrayed as whole persons instead of the traditionally stereotyped ones.

If the students have worked through these various activities, they should see that the barriers placed around both sexes concerning roles and behavior create restrictions which hinder each sex in perceiving for themselves what it means to be masculine or feminine.

Incorporating the Study of Sex-Role Stereotyping into Existing Programs

Marylyn E. Calabrese
Project Director
"Becoming Sex-Blind: The Tredyffrin/Easttown Project"

The author details ideas for launching students into a study of sex roles, including using the "Baby X" story. This exercise is easily adaptable for all grade levels.

Making students aware of the effects of sex-role stereotyping is a task that can begin anywhere. It need not encompass an entire unit, although such a project may certainly be desirable. Rather, students can assimilate an examination of this subject alongside of and in regular classroom units. There are several advantages to such an approach: it allows the student time to reflect when activities are spread over an entire semester or year; also, short, frequent activities may be more acceptable to some students who, at first, may consider the subject lacking in academic merit. The purpose of this article will be to identify some ways in which existing programs and units can include segments on sex-role stereotyping.

I. Storytelling: Teaching Boys, Girls, and "Xes"

Entitled "X: A Fabulous Child's Story," (Lois Gould, *Ms.* Magazine, December 1972), the story of Baby X is excellent reading for "children" of all ages. The point of the story is simply this: gender is irrelevant to the educational process. Filled with humor and suspense, the story, which I usually read aloud to my students, is successful in raising several key questions. From birth to puberty, how important is a person's sex in the childrearing/socialization process? Secondly, what if—and it's a *fabulous* "if,"—what if we did not know the sex of a child who is assigned to our classroom? How *would* we treat this person?

Synopsis: In a secret governmental experiment, Ms. and Mr. Jones become the parents of a child, whose sex is known only to them. Deprived of this "crucial" information, friends and relatives argue over the baby's name, clothes, toys. No one knows quite what to do. Except the parents, that is, who are informed by the Instruction Manual to give both cuddling and rough and tumble play. When Baby X enters school, the problems raised by teachers, and other kids and their parents, increase considerably.

5

Eventually, the parents of the other children, disturbed when children like Janie and Johnny begin to bake cakes, do needlepoint, or enter the science fair and play football, pressure the principal to call in a psychiatrist to examine Baby X. The ending, which I won't reveal here, is a delightful surprise, and stimulates discussion on the many harmful effects of sex-role stereotyping.

Questions of followup discussion:

1. As the story was being read, how did you picture Baby X? (Many insist a boy, others a girl. The reasons they give can be very interesting.)
2. What does the ending mean?
3. How do you account for the actions of the adults? Although the students eventually accepted Baby X, why did the parents have a harder time?
4. What are some of the consequences of rigid sex-role stereotyping, as evidenced in the story?
5. Identify any of the ways boys and girls are treated differently in school in the story. Compare them to your school.
6. The story portrays most children's toys as sexist. Bring in some examples of ads, packaging, etc. which confirm this. Can you find some that do not?
7. In reading the story aloud, one can read through to the end, or stop before the psychiatrist's report and have the class speculate on all the possible endings. (Rarely do they guess the real one.) Some students like to create their own endings, giving reasons for their choices. Acting out and role-playing are also possible. (*Comment:* Because the story is so short [less than six pages], it can be read aloud, or teachers may wish to obtain the publisher's permission to reproduce it on ditto or photocopy machine. It can be used as a single activity to raise awareness and discussion, or as the introduction to a longer unit. Frankly, I often use it as a "day before vacation" treat. Any grade level is possible, senior or junior high, even elementary. When read aloud, it is truly a story for everyone. The reading and discussion can fit easily into one class period.

II. What Is Your Sexism Quotient?: Questions for Consciousness Raising

These questions, written by high school students, reflect THEIR— as opposed to OUR—concerns on the effects of sex-role stereotyping.

Girls
1. Do you ever play dumb around boys? Why?
2. Do you consider marriage and children as your ultimate fulfillment in

life? Will you be a failure if you don't achieve these?
3. Do you think boys should be more sexually experienced than girls?
4. Would you rather be unusually brilliant or unusually beautiful?
5. Have you ever changed plans with your best girl friend for a date with a boy? Any boy?
6. Are you willing to pay for some dates?
7. Must a boy "take you somewhere" on a date?
8. How do you feel about your boyfriend having other girls for friends?
9. Do you object to washing windows? the car? taking out trash? mowing the lawn?
10. What does women's liberation mean to you?

Boys
1. To what extent do you think of girls in terms of "making it"?
2. How do you feel if a girl you like is smarter than you are?
3. Would you mind working for a female boss?
4. Do you consider marriage and children as your ultimate fulfillment in life? Will you be a failure if you don't achieve these?
5. Would you rather be unusually brilliant or unusually handsome?
6. Does it bother you if the girl chips in on a date? if she takes the initiative on a date?
7. How do you feel about your girlfriend having other boys for friends?
8. Do you prefer girls to wear skirts?
9. Do you object to doing the dishes? cooking dinner? cleaning the house?
10. Do you know how women's liberation benefits men?

COMMENT: A variety of procedures can be used depending on the group. Same-sex groupings followed by mixed total class discussion works very well. Sometimes a whole period may be spent on one or two questions, depending on the interests of the students. The last time I used the exercise, many students commented that the division into boys' questions and girls' questions was artificial, and that they wanted one list! You may want to experiment with one list for some groups, a divided one for others. Because these questions involve the students' personal lives, family patterns, etc., be prepared for some strong reactions, embarrassment, fervor, or whatever.

III. Topics, Topics, and More Topics

When was the last time you gave a list of topics to a class in connection with an assignment?

Of course, it's something we do all the time for literature papers, personal essays, debate topics, etc. One of the easiest ways to incorporate the subject of sex-role stereotyping into your existing classroom plans is by jogging the imaginations of your speakers, readers, and writers with subjects on the entire spectrum of the women's rights movement, human liberation, sex-role socialization. By doing this, not only will you be impressing on your students that this is a subject worthy of serious academic study and, therefore, of their consideration, but you will also succeed in broadening their scope of the subject beyond the limited representation frequently given by the media. An additional bonus to this type of approach is that the librarians of your school may be motivated to add more nonsexist materials to their collection in order to meet the requests of your students.

Possible topic areas

Writing research papers. The last time I announced to an Advanced Writing class that they were to research an important figure in American history, I passed over my initial impulse to include the old warhorses Lincoln, Roosevelt, John Adams, etc. and instead read from the assignment sheet the names of Sojourner Truth, Mercy Otis Warren, Harriet Tubman, Susan B. Anthony, Elizabeth Cady Stanton, and Alice Paul, with the same inflection and the same authority as if I had announced those other names. The reaction was immediate and strong. After much confusion about who these women were, many students questioned how these historical figures could have been important if so little was known about them. Several students elected them for research.

Writing personal essays. Drawing on their own experiences as well as those of others, students can explore such topics as the androgynous person, or advantages/drawbacks to being a girl/boy. One of my favorites is to assign girls, "What it means to be a boy," and give boys the counterpart topic on girls. When papers are exchanged, students begin to separate stereotype from reality.

Debate topics and speeches. The Equal Rights Amendment and coed sports teams are not the only topics available, although they are certainly worthwhile ones. But why limit yourself to the old standbys? How about 1) women in management; 2) sexism in your history text; or 3) the double standard of mental health? The possibilities are many.

Literature. "The Portrayal of Men in *Deliverance* (James Dickey)" is a good topic for a literary analysis paper. Here is an instance where the subject of sex stereotyping in a work refers especially to men. Lewis, with his macho personality, raises many questions on the topic, "What is masculinity?"

Reading Nonfiction. Recently, in connection with a unit on nonfiction, I assigned the reading of two nonfiction articles with these limitations: the articles had to be on topics of current interest and found in popular magazines. Along with multiple issues of *The Sunday New York Times Magazine, Time, Psychology Today* and *Philadelphia Magazine*, I also provided copies of *Womensports* and *Ms.* magazines. By simply having materials available, no additional comment or direction is necessary. (*Comment*: Enlist the cooperation of the school librarian.)

IV. The Portrayal of Women in —————————.

You fill in the blank with your favorite novel, poem, or play. Along with your regular study of a particular work, some time can be devoted to the author's image of women.

For an extended discussion and analysis, as well as for an excellent comparison with the contemporary woman, I fill in the blank with Chaucer's *The Canterbury Tales*, notably the so-called "Marriage Group": "The Wife of Bath's Prologue and Tale," the "Clerk's Tale," and the "Franklin's Tale." When Chaucer raises the question of what women want in marriage, the possibilities for contemporary parallels are numerous, ranging from woman as dominant (Wife of Bath), to women as doormat (patient Griselda in the Clerk's Tale), to woman as equal person (the Franklin's Tale.) (*Comment*: Many students find *The Canterbury Tales*, even in modern verse translation [I use the Nevill Coghill version], difficult reading. Also, the subject matter is such that a more mature class would get the maximum enjoyment from such a study. One week [out of a longer unit on Chaucer] can accommodate this segment adequately.)

V. Potpourri

A little of this, a little of that, is exactly what editor Betsy Ryan promises in the paperback *The Sexes: Male/Female Roles and Relationships* (Scholastic Book Services, $1.25, 1975, 186 pages). Similar to Bantam's *Dig USA* series, it gives students a taste of the various ways that sex-role stereotyping can affect their lives. Presenting a wide range of views on male and female roles, the book includes poems, articles, cartoons, opinion polls, photographs, advertisements, and even quotations of feminist Gloria Steinem juxtaposed with those of male supremacist Lionel Tiger.

The first section, "Male and Female," (65 pages) is the best and well worth the purchase price of the book. (The other sections, "Courtship," "Love," and "Marriage," are, in my opinion, somewhat limited in that they focus on traditional stereotypes.) In the first part, high school students give their views, both pro and con, on the women's liberation movement; there is an excellent short essay, "Making It in a Man's World," showing a young woman's perspective of the legal profession, first as a law student and later as a practicing attorney; and there are Dear Abby excerpts, James Thurber cartoons, and poetry selections by Mari Evans ("I am a black woman") and Sylvia Plath ("In Plaster"). (*Comment*: This is a useful resource for an entire unit or shorter assignments on sex-role stereotyping. Use the ads, photographs, and opinion polls with a unit on the media. The entire book includes thirty-four poems; there is plenty of choice for a good poetry unit. Especially well suited to the low ability student, the selections are short, very readable, and high in interest motivation. One drawback, however, is that unless you have multiple copies of the book, you may find it difficult to duplicate some of the excerpts. Because of the great variety of the selections, the book can be used with both junior and senior high students.)

X: A FABULOUS CHILD'S STORY
by Lois Gould

Once upon a time, a baby named X was born. This baby was named X so that nobody could tell whether it was a boy or a girl. Its parents could tell, of course, but they couldn't tell anybody else. They couldn't even tell Baby X, at first.

You see, it was all part of a very important Secret Scientific Xperiment, known officially as Project Baby X. The smartest scientists had set up this Xperiment at a cost of Xactly 23 billion dollars and 72 cents, which might seem like a lot for just one baby, even a very important Xperimental baby. But when you remember the prices of things like strained carrots and stuffed bunnies, and popcorn for the movies and booster shots for camp, let along 28 shiny quarters from the tooth fairy, you begin to see how it adds up.

Also, long before Baby X was born, all those scientists had to be paid to work out the details of the Xperiment, and to write the *Official Instruction Manual* for Baby X's parents and, most important of all, to find the right set of parents to bring up Baby X. These parents had to be selected very carefully. Thousands of volunteers had to take thousands of tests and answer thousands of tricky questions. Almost everybody failed because, it turned out, almost everybody really wanted either a baby boy or a baby girl, and not Baby X at all. Also, almost everybody was afraid that a Baby X would be a lot more trouble than a boy or a girl. (They were probably right, the scientists admitted, but Baby X needed parents who wouldn't *mind* the Xtra trouble.)

There were families with grandparents named Milton and Agatha, who didn't see why the baby couldn't be named Milton or Agatha instead of X, even if it *was* an X. There were families with aunts who insisted on knitting tiny dresses and uncles who insisted on sending tiny baseball mitts. Worst of all, there were families that already had other children who couldn't be trusted to keep the secret. Certainly not if they knew the secret was worth 23 billion dollars and 72 cents—and all you had to do was take one little peek at Baby X in the bathtub to know if it was a boy or a girl.

But, finally, the scientists found the Joneses, who really wanted to raise an X more than any other kind of baby—no matter how much trouble it would be. Ms. and Mr. Jones had to promise they would take equal turns caring for X, and feeding it, and singing it lullabies. And they had to promise never to hire any baby-sitters. The government scientists knew perfectly well that a baby-sitter would probably peek at X in the bathtub, too.

The day the Joneses brought their baby home, lots of friends and relatives came over to see it. None of them knew about the secret Xperiment, though. So the first thing they asked was what kind of a baby X was. When the Joneses smiled and said, "It's an X!" nobody knew what to say. They couldn't say, "Look at her cute little dimples!" And they couldn't say, "Look at his husky little biceps!" And they couldn't even say just plain "kitchy-coo." In fact, they all thought the Joneses were playing some kind of rude joke.

But, of course, the Joneses were not joking. "It's an X" was absolutely all they would say. And that made the friends and relatives very angry. The relatives all felt embarrassed about having an X in the family. "People will think there's something wrong with it!" some of them whispered. "There *is* something wrong with it!" others whispered back.

"Nonsense!" the Joneses told them all cheerfully. "What could possibly be wrong with this perfectly adorable X?"

Nobody could answer that, except Baby X, who had just finished its bottle. Baby X's answer was a loud, satisfied burp.

Clearly, nothing at all was wrong. Nevertheless, none of the relatives felt comfortable about buying a present for a Baby X. The cousins who sent the baby a tiny football helmet would not come and visit any more. And the neighbors who sent a pink-flowered romper suit pulled their shades down when the Joneses passed their house.

The *Official Instruction Manual* had warned the new parents that this would happen, so they didn't fret about it. Besides, they were too busy with Baby X and the hundreds of different Xercises for treating it properly.

Ms. and Mr. Jones had to be Xtra careful about how they played with little X. They knew that if they kept bouncing it up in the air and saying how *strong* and *active* it was, they'd be treating it more like a boy than an X. But if all they did was cuddle it and kiss it and tell it how *sweet* and *dainty* it was, they'd be treating it more like a girl than an X.

On page 1,654 of the *Official Instruction Manual*, the scientists prescribed: "plenty of bouncing and plenty of cuddling, *both*. X ought to be strong and sweet and active. Forget about *dainty* altogether."

Meanwhile, the Joneses were worrying about other problems. Toys, for instance. And clothes. On his first shopping trip, Mr. Jones told the store clerk, "I need some clothes and toys for my new baby." The clerk smiled and said, "Well, now, is it a boy or a girl?" "It's an X," Mr. Jones said, smiling back. But the clerk got all red in the face and said huffily, "In *that* case, I'm afraid I can't help you, sir." So Mr. Jones wandered helplessly up and down the aisles trying to find what X needed. But everything in the store was piled up in sections marked "Boys" or "Girls." There were "Boys' Pajamas" and "Girls' Underwear" and "Boys' Fire Engines" and "Girls' Housekeeping Sets." Mr. Jones went home without buying anything for X. That night he and Ms. Jones consulted page 2,326 of the *Official Instruction Manual*. "Buy plenty of everything!" it said firmly.

So they bought plenty of sturdy blue pajamas in the Boys' Department and cheerful flowered underwear in the Girls' Department. And they bought all kinds of toys. A boy doll that made pee-pee and cried, "Pa-pa." And a girl doll that talked in three languages and said, "I am the Pres-i-dent of Gen-er-al Mo-tors." They also bought a storybook about a brave princess who rescued a handsome prince from his ivory tower, and another one about a sister and brother who grew up to be a baseball star and a ballet star, and you had to guess which was which.

The head scientists of Project Baby X checked all their purchases and told them to keep up the good work. They also reminded the Joneses to see page 4,629 of the *Manual*, where it said, "Never make Baby X feel *embarrassed* or *ashamed* about what it wants to play with. And if X gets dirty climbing rocks, never say 'Nice little Xes don't get dirty climbing rocks.'"

Likewise, it said, "If X falls down and cries, never say 'Brave little Xes don't cry.' Because, of course, nice little Xes *do* get dirty, and brave little Xes *do* cry. No matter how dirty X gets, or how hard it cries, don't worry. It's all part of the Xperiment."

Whenever the Joneses pushed Baby X's stroller in the park, smiling strangers would come over and coo: "Is that a boy or girl?" The Joneses would smile back and say, "It's an X." The strangers would stop smiling then, and often snarl something nasty—as if the Joneses had snarled at *them.*

By the time X grew big enough to play with other children, the Joneses' troubles had grown bigger, too. Once a little girl grabbed X's shovel in the sandbox, and zonked X on the head with it. "Now, now, Tracy," the little girl's mother began to scold, "little girls mustn't hit little—" and she turned to ask X, "Are you a little boy or a little girl, dear?"

Mr. Jones, who was sitting near the sandbox, held his breath and crossed his fingers.

X smiled politely at the lady, even though X's head had never been zonked so hard in its life. "I'm a little X," X replied.

"You're a *what?*" the lady exclaimed angrily. "You're a little b-r-a-t, you mean!"

"But little girls mustn't hit little Xes, either!" said X, retrieving the shovel with another polite smile. "What good does hitting do, anyway?"

X's father, who was still holding his breath, finally let it out, uncrossed his fingers, and grinned back at X.

And at their next secret Project Baby X meeting, the scientists grinned, too. Baby X was doing fine.

But then it was time for X to start school. The Joneses were really worried about this, because school was even more full of rules for boys and girls, and there were no rules for Xes. The teacher would tell boys to form one line, and girls to form another line. There would be boys' games and girls' games, and boys' secrets and girls' secrets. The school library would have a list of recommended books for girls, and a different list of recommended books for boys. There would even be a bathroom marked BOYS and another one marked GIRLS. Pretty soon boys and girls would hardly talk to each other. What would happen to poor little X?

The Joneses spent weeks consulting their *Instruction Manual* (there were 249½ pages of advice under "First Day of School"), and attending urgent special conferences with the smart scientists of Project Baby X.

The scientists had to make sure that X's mother had taught X how to throw and catch a ball properly, and that X's father had been sure to teach X what to serve at a doll's tea party. X had to know how to shoot marbles and how to jump rope and, most of all, what to say when the Other Children asked whether X was a Boy or a Girl.

Finally, X was ready. The Joneses helped X button on a nice new pair of red-and-white checked overalls, and sharpened six pencils for X's nice new pencilbox, and marked X's name clearly on all the books in its nice new bookbag. X brushed its teeth and combed its hair, which just about covered its ears, and remembered to put a napkin in its lunchbox.

The Joneses had asked X's teacher if the class could line up alphabetically, instead of forming separate lines for boys and girls. And they had asked if X could use the principal's bathroom, because it wasn't marked anything except BATH-ROOM. X's teacher promised to take care of all those problems. But nobody could help X with the biggest problem of all—Other Children.

Nobody in X's class had ever known an X before. What would they think? How would X make friends?

You couldn't tell what X was by studying its clothes—overalls don't even button right-to-left, like girls' clothes, or left-to-right, like boys' clothes. And you couldn't guess whether X had a girl's short haircut or a boy's long haircut. And it was very hard to tell by the games X liked to play. Either X played ball very well for a girl, or else X played house very well for a boy.

Some of the children tried to find out by asking X tricky questions, like "Who's your favorite sports star?" That was easy. X had two favorite sports stars: a girl jockey named Robyn Smith and a boy archery champion named Robin Hood. Then they asked, "What's your favorite TV program?" And that was even easier. X's favorite TV program was "Lassie," which stars a girl dog played by a boy dog.

When X said that its favorite toy was a doll, everyone decided that X must be a girl. But then X said that the doll was really a robot, and that X has computerized it, and that it was programmed to bake fudge brownies and then clean up the kitchen. After X told them that, the other children gave up guessing what X was. All they knew was they'd sure like to see X's doll.

After school, X wanted to play with the other children. "How about shooting some baskets in the gym?" X asked the girls. But all they did was make faces and giggle behind X's back.

"How about weaving some baskets in the arts and crafts room?" X asked the boys. But they all made faces and giggled behind X's back, too.

That night, Ms. and Mr. Jones asked X how things had gone at school. X told them sadly that the lessons were okay, but otherwise school was a terrible place for an X. It seemed as if Other Children would never want an X for a friend.

Once more, the Joneses reached for their *Instruction Manual*. Under "Other Children," they found the following message: "What did you Xpect? *Other Children* have to obey all the silly boy-girl rules, because their parents taught them to. Lucky X—you don't have to stick to the rules at all! All you have to do is be yourself. P.S. We're not saying it'll be easy."

X like being itself. But X cried a lot that night, partly because it felt afraid. So X's father held X tight, and cuddled it, and couldn't help crying a little, too. And X's mother cheered them both up by reading an Xciting story about an enchanted prince called Sleeping Handsome, who woke up when Princess Charming kissed him.

The next morning, they all felt much better, and little X went back to school with a brave smile and a clean pair of red-and-white checked overalls.

There was a seven-letter-word spelling bee in class that day. And a seven-lap boys' relay race in the gym. And a seven-layer-cake baking contest in the girls' kitchen corner. X won the spelling bee. X also won the relay race. And X almost won the baking contest, except it forgot to light the oven. Which only proves that nobody's perfect.

One of the Other Children noticed something else, too. He said: "Winning or losing doesn't seem to count to X. X seems to have fun being good at boys' skills *and* girls' skills."

"Come to think of it," said another one of the Other Children, "maybe X is having twice as much fun as we are!"

So after school that day, the girl who beat X at the baking contest gave X a big slice of her prizewinning cake. And the boy X beat in the relay race asked X to race him home.

From then on, some really funny things began to happen. Susie, who sat next to X in class, suddenly refused to wear pink dresses to school any more. She insisted on wearing red-and-white checked overalls—just like X's. Overalls, she told her parents, were much better for climbing monkey bars.

Then Jim, the class football nut, started wheeling his little sister's doll carriage around the football field. He'd put on his entire football uniform, except for the helmet. Then he'd put the helmet *in* the carriage, lovingly tucked under an old set of shoulder pads. Then he'd start jogging around the field, pushing the carriage and singing "Rockabye Baby" to his football helmet. He told his family that X did the same thing, so it must be okay. After all, X was now the team's star quarterback.

Susie's parents were horrified by her behavior, and Jim's parents were worried sick about his. But the worst came when the twins, Joe and Peggy, decided to share everything with each other. Peggy used Joe's hockey skates, and his microscope, and took half his newspaper route. Joe used Peggy's needlepoint kit, and her cookbooks, and took two of her three baby-sitting jobs. Peggy started running the lawn mower, and Joe started running the vacuum cleaner.

Their parents weren't one bit pleased with Peggy's wonderful biology experiments, or with Joe's terrific needlepoint pillows. They didn't care that Peggy mowed the lawn better, and that Joe vacuumed the carpet better. In fact, they were furious. It's all that little X's fault, they agreed. Just because X doesn't know what it is, or what it's supposed to be, it wants to get everybody *else* mixed up, too!

Peggy and Joe were forbidden to play with X any more. So was Susie, and then Jim, and then *all* the Other Children. But it was too late; the Other Children stayed mixed up and happy and free, and refused to go back to the way they'd been before X.

Finally, Joe and Peggy's parents decided to call an emergency meeting of the school's Parents' Association, to discuss "The X Problem." They sent a report to the principal stating that X was a "disruptive influence." They demanded immediate action. The Joneses, they said, should be *forced* to tell whether X was a boy or a girl. And then X should be *forced* to behave like whichever it was. If the Joneses refused to tell, the Parents' Association said, then X must take an Xamination. The school psychiatrist must Xamine it physically and mentally, and issue a full report. If X's test showed it was a boy, it would have to obey all the boys' rules. If it proved to be a girl, X would have to obey all the girls' rules.

And if X turned out to be some kind of mixed-up misfit, then X should be Xpelled from the school. Immediately!

The principal was very upset. Disruptive influence? Mixed-up misfit? But X was an Xcellent student. All the teachers said it was a delight to have X in their classes. X was president of the student council. X had won first prize in the talent show, and second prize in the art show, and honorable mention in the science fair, and six athletic events on field day, including the potato race.

Nevertheless, insisted the Parents' Association, X is a Problem Child. X is the Biggest Problem Child we have ever seen!

So the principal reluctantly notified X's parents that numerous complaints about X's behavior had come to the school's attention. And that after the psychiatrist's Xamination, the school would decide what to do about X.

The Joneses reported this at once to the scientists, who referred them to page 85,759 of the *Instruction Manual.* "Sooner or later," it said, "X will have to be Xamined by a psychiatrist. This may be the only way any of us will know for sure whether X is mixed up—or whether everyone else is."

The night before X was to be Xamined, the Joneses tried not to let X see how worried they were. "What if—?" Mr. Jones would say. And Ms. Jones would reply, "No use worrying." Then a few minutes later, Ms. Jones would say, "What if—?" and Mr. Jones would reply, "No use worrying."

X just smiled at them both, and hugged them hard and didn't say much of anything. X was thinking, What if—? And then X thought: No use worrying.

At Xactly 9 o'clock the next day, X reported to the school psychiatrist's office. The principal, along with a committee from the Parents' Association, X's teacher, X's classmates, and Ms. and Mr. Jones, waited in the hall outside. Nobody knew the details of the tests X was to be given, but everybody knew they'd be *very* hard, and that they'd reveal Xactly what everyone wanted to know about X, but were afraid to ask.

It was terribly quiet in the hall. Almost spooky. Once in a while, they would hear a strange noise inside the room. There were buzzes. And a beep or two. And several bells. An occasional light would flash under the door. The Joneses thought it was a white light, but the principal thought it was blue. Two or three children swore it was either yellow or green. And the Parents' Committee missed it completely.

Through it all, you could hear the psychiatrist's low voice, asking hundreds of questions, and X's higher voice, answering hundreds of answers.

The whole thing took so long that everyone knew it must be the most complete Xamination anyone had ever had to take. Poor X, the Joneses thought. Serves X right, the Parents' Committee thought. I wouldn't like to be in X's overalls right now, the children thought.

At last, the door opened. Everyone crowded around to hear the results. X didn't look any different; in fact, X was smiling. But the psychiatrist looked terrible. He looked as if he was crying! "What happened?" everyone began shouting. Had X done something disgraceful? "I wouldn't be a bit surprised!" muttered Peggy and Joe's parents. "Did X flunk the *whole* test?" cried Susie's parents. "Or just the most important part?" yelled Jim's parents.

"Oh, dear," sighed Mr. Jones.

"Oh, dear," sighed Ms. Jones.

"*Sssh,*" ssshed the principal. "The psychiatrist is trying to speak."

Wiping his eyes and clearing his throat, the psychiatrist began, in a hoarse whisper. "In my opinion," he whispered—you could tell he must be very upset—"in my opinion, young X here—"

"Yes? Yes?" shouted a parent impatiently.

"*Sssh!*" ssshed the principal.

"Young *Sssh* here, I mean young X," said the doctor, frowning, "is just about—"

"Just about *what*? Let's have it!" shouted another parent.

"... just about the *least* mixed-up child I've ever Xamined!" said the psychiatrist.

"Yay for X!" yelled one of the children. And then the others began yelling, too. Clapping and cheering and jumping up and down.

"*SSSH!*" SSShed the principal, but nobody did.

The Parents' Committee was angry and bewildered. How *could* X have passed the whole Xamination? Didn't X have an *identity* problem? Wasn't X mixed up at *all*? Wasn't X *any* kind of a misfit? How could it *not* be, when it didn't even *know* what it was? And why was the psychiatrist crying?

Actually, he had stopped crying and was smiling politely through his tears. "Don't you see?" he said. "I'm crying because it's wonderful! X has absolutely no identity problem! X isn't one bit mixed up! As for being a misfit—ridiculous! X knows perfectly well what it is! Don't you, X?" The doctor winked. X winked back.

"But what *is* X?" shrieked Peggy and Joe's parents. "*We* still want to know what it is!"

"Ah, yes," said the doctor, winking again. "Well, don't worry. You'll all know one of these days. And you won't need me to tell you."

"What? What does he mean?" some of the parents grumbled suspiciously.

Susie and Peggy and Joe all answered at once. "He means that by the time X's sex matters, it won't be a secret any more!"

With that, the doctor began to push through the crowd toward X's parents. "How do you do," he said, somewhat stiffly. And then he reached out to hug them both. "If I ever have an X of my own," he whispered, "I sure hope you'll lend me your instruction manual."

Needless to say, the Joneses were very happy. The Project Baby X scientists were rather pleased, too. So were Susie, Jim, Peggy, Joe, and all the Other Children. The Parents' Association wasn't, but they had promised to accept the psychiatrist's report, and not make any more trouble. They even invited Ms. and Mr. Jones to become honorary members, which they did.

Later that day, all X's friends put on their red-and-white checked overalls and went over to see X. They found X in the back yard, playing with a very tiny baby that none of them have ever seen before. The baby was wearing very tiny red-and-white checked overalls.

"How do you like our new baby?" X asked the Other Children proudly.

"It's got cute dimples," said Jim.

"It's got husky biceps, too," said Susie.

"What kind of baby is it?" asked Joe and Peggy.

X frowned at them. "Can't you tell?" Then X broke into a big, mischievous grin. *"It's a Y!"*

Recognizing Sex-Role Stereotyping

Judith A. Noble
University of Akron
Akron, Ohio

*An undergraduate class in children's literature
recognized sex-role stereotyping during a small
group project built around a random selection
of picture books about children.*

Recognition of a problem or situation is necessarily a prerequisite to effecting any change in attitude or teaching practices. Having found through discussions that many of my undergraduate children's literature students were either unaware of sex-role stereotyping in books, or unconcerned because they felt the reports were greatly biased, I developed the following activity to promote recognition of the situation.

Since the students in this class ordinarily work in small groups for discussion, there are usually 3-5 groups completing the activity and then comparing results.

Following is the outline which each group is given for guidance:

Outline of Activity

Topic: Sex Roles in Children's Picture Books

Materials: Lenore J. Weitzman et al., "Sex-Role Socialization in Picture Books for Preschool Children," *American Journal of Sociology*, 77 (1972): 1125-1150; 10 picture books with children as main characters, randomly selected.

Procedures

1. Read the article.
2. Read the 10 picture books.
3. Categorize the sex roles displayed by these children.
4. What conclusions can you reach about the sex roles portrayed in these books?
5. Do your conclusions support or refute the arguments presented in the article? Give examples from the books.
6. Some people contend that these books are damaging to the self-concept of both girls and boys. Others disagree saying that children are influenced by real people rather than books. How do you feel? Why?

To begin the activity in an obviously unbiased manner, two students from each group go to the picture book shelves in the library and indicate a beginning book. They then take the next ten books which have children as main characters. (The books are *not* shelved alphabetically by author, so the chances of their picking more than one book by an author are slight.) Meanwhile, the other members of the group have been summarizing the article, a report of a content analysis of sex roles in Caldecott Medal books and Little Golden Books.

This analysis showed that females are largely invisible and that when they do appear they are usually not the main characters. Boys are depicted as active leaders while girls are depicted as passive followers; females are usually in traditional roles aimed at pleasing or serving males. A frequent reaction to this article is disbelief. Having heard for many years that books are aimed at girls, many students are unwilling to accept the evidence. For this reason, the second part of the activity, looking at randomly selected picture books for sex stereotyping, was included.

The picture books are then read aloud by group members and each is discussed regarding portrayed sex roles, numbers of girls and boys, behavior patterns, dress, occupations, etc. These results are then compared to the conclusions of the article.

A few discussion questions are provided for guidance. However, the students usually become very involved in the discussion and questions evolve as they go along. The most frequently heard question is a dismayed "Why do they [the authors] do this?"

It is usually found that eight or nine of the ten picture books have the same characteristics as were reported in the content analysis. Even though ten books is a small sample from which to draw a conclusion, the fact that each group arrives at the same conclusion independently tends to support their findings.

I have found this activity to be beneficial both in promoting awareness of the situation and in provoking discussion among group members. It is not unusual to find the critical thinking skills fostered by this activity extending into the other activities in the class.

Changing Children's Attitudes toward Sex Roles

Alice L. Muir
White Oak School
McKeesport, Pennsylvania

Using a questionnaire for diagnosis of sex-role attitudes and evaluation of her project, the author chose fifteen selections to read aloud and discuss with four sixth-grade classes.

"A woman should be kindhearted," said the Great Spirit, who had come to Earth disguised as a poor old man. The remark was made to a wicked old woman who had refused him a piece of cake. She had to be punished, and so he stamped his foot, and her body diminished and transformed until she flew out the window as the first woodpecker. Thus, another triumph of male dominance occurred as the woman was banished to a life in the trees.

My sixth-grade class and I were discussing this story from a workbook page (Houghton Mifflin, *Bright Peaks*, 1966, p. 25), designed to enhance students' skill in using contextual clues, and I asked them, "What is wrong with the statement, 'A woman should be kindhearted'?" Blank stares. I tried again. "Is there anything in that sentence that could be changed?" There was silence, and finally someone ventured the opinion that both women and men should be kindhearted. Discussion followed, and it was clear to me that sexual stereotypes abounded in that class. The majority of students felt that boys should not cry and that certain occupations are exclusively for males and others definitely for females. I sensed a need for the introduction of nonsexist curriculum material if there was to be a change in their apparent attitudes.

Research on changing attitudes with regard to sexism is in the early stages. In an article in *Mediacenter*, Sprung reported that Puffer (1975) engaged in a study designed to measure the changes in a fourth-grade class after exposure to a nonsexist curriculum. The curriculum included the use of puppets, career education, and field trips into the community. Pretests and posttests were used to measure attitudinal changes; early results have indicated that some measurable changes did occur. Since the data have not yet been entirely computed, the statistics from the study cannot be reported.

There has been considerable research, however, on changing racial attitudes by the implementation of curriculum materials stressing the accomplishments of blacks. Recent research studies support the idea that curriculum content does affect children's racial attitudes. Litcher and Johnson (1969), Johnson (1966), Roth (1969), Georgeoff (1967), and Gezi and Johnson (1970) have all reported on the effectiveness of curriculum materials in effecting attitudinal change.

Confident, then, that curriculum can be a vital force in changing attitudes, I designed a test to assess what the students' attitudes were toward suitability of the sexes for various occupations. The questionnarie included fifteen items related to occupations and one item that concerned a playtime activity.

QUESTIONNAIRE

1. What do you think would be the better first name for a person who delivers the mail?

    Bob   Jane   Either one

2. What do you think would be the better first name for a doctor?

    Bob   Jane   Either one

3. What do you think would be the better first name for a secretary?

    Bob   Jane   Either one

4. What do you think would be the better first name for the president of a country?

    Bob   Jane   Either one

5. What do you think would be the better first name for a judge?

    Bob   Jane   Either one

6. What do you think would be the better first name for a nurse?

    Bob   Jane   Either one

7. What do you think would be the better first name for a veterinarian?

       Bob   Jane   Either one

8. What do you think would be the better first name for a writer?

       Bob   Jane   Either one

9. What do you think would be the better first name for a person who drives a dump truck?

       Bob   Jane   Either one

10. What do you think would be the better first name for a pilot?

       Bob   Jane   Either one

11. What do you think would be the better first name for a teacher?

       Bob   Jane   Either one

12. What do you think would be the better first name for a surgeon?

       Bob   Jane   Either one

13. What do you think would be the better first name for a lawyer?

       Bob   Jane   Either one

14. What do you think would be the better first name for a poet?

       Bob   Jane   Either one

15. What do you think would be the better first name for a person who works in an office building?

       Bob   Jane   Either one

16. What do you think would be the better first name for a person who plays with dolls?

       Bob   Jane   Either one

A response of "Either one" was deemed as representing a nonsexist attitude. Either of the other responses, Bob or Jane, was considered sexist.

The study was limited to my 121 sixth-grade students. The school is located in a middle-class suburb with a predominantly white population. The questionnaire was administered as a pretest. I read orally all sixteen items to the four sixth-grade sections to negate the influence of reading ability on the responses to the items. Results were tabulated, and the totals are shown in Table 1.

Table 1

Totals Selecting Each of the Three Responses—Pretest

Group	Bob	Jane	Either one
A	172	124	200
B	180	125	175
C	143	126	227
D	171	115	178

Since Group B contained the fewest number of "either one" responses, I selected Group B as the Experimental group, and the other three sections served as control groups.

Curriculum content was a major concern of mine. From *Images of*

Women, published by the Pennsylvania Department of Education in 1973, and more recent publications from our school library, I was able to compile a list of books that would serve as the content for the study. I was now ready to begin.

For the first day of the experiment I decided to read Stan and Jan Berenstain's *He Bear She Bear* to the class. I had made the decision to read the books orally to the experimental group not only to ensure that they were read, but also because the students looked forward to my reading to them in the few months we had been together, and I wanted this to be an enjoyable experience for all. I was a bit apprehensive about their reaction to *He Bear She Bear*, and so I first discussed with them the famous Berenstain Bear family and showed the Random House filmstrip *The Bear Scouts*, based on another Berenstain Bear book. I then introduced and read the newest of this series of books, *He Bear She Bear*, which portrays male and female bears in traditional and nontraditional roles. Together we searched the pictures for what the he bear and she bear were doing. Several students asked to look at the book after class, and the study was begun!

The next book we read was Norma Klein's *Girls Can Be Anything*. This delightful story tells of Adam Sobel and his best friend in kindergarten, Marina. Marina is not content to enact traditional feminine roles and challenges Adam on his desire to make her the nurse instead of the doctor, the stewardess instead of the pilot, the president's wife instead of the president, in their play together. Marina's parents assist her in her nontraditional thinking, assuring her that she is right.

Two books similar in content were read the next day: *Mommies at Work* by Eve Merriam and *Mothers Can Do Anything* by Joe Lasker. To bring to their attention her role as a poet, I told the students that Eve Merriam would be a very familiar name to them in a few months when we finished our unit on poetry. As I read *Mommies at Work*, I asked how many students' mothers had jobs doing any of the things mentioned in the book. A few students did have mothers who were cashiers, teachers, and clerks in stores, and we talked about the fact that even though none of their mothers were employed at many of the jobs in the book, there are mothers who do have jobs in circuses, on assembly lines, and in laboratories. The students enjoyed the many colorful pictures in Lasker's book. The last one, showing a woman astronaut floating in air, seemed of particular interest to them, and we discussed how soon we thought it would be before a spacecraft was launched with a woman astronaut aboard.

On the next two days I read to them the *What Can She Be?* books of Gloria and Esther Goldreich. The first read was *What Can She Be? A Veterinarian*, which presents a day in the life of a veterinarian named Dr. Penny. The pictures in the book of various animals at the vet's are extremely good, and the students responded enthusiastically to the book and its pictures. In fact, the next day I was besieged with requests from one of the control groups to read them the book about the vet. The following day I read *What Can She Be? A Lawyer*. This book introduces young people to the legal profession as Ellen's experiences with various interesting legal problems are recounted. One student said she was surprised that lawyers did more than defend persons accused of crimes.

Ann Can Fly by Fred Phleger was the next book the experimental group heard. This story relates experiences in the life of Ann and her father as they fly to her summer camp in her father's plane. There is much information given about planning flights; the highlight of the story is Ann's exciting brief experience in flying the plane herself under Father's watchful eye.

One of the least popular books was *Boys and Girls, Girls and Boys* by Eve Merriam, which details the activities of some boys and girls who are free of traditional sex role behavior.

Over the ensuing days I read selections from a collection of stories called *Women Themselves* by Johanna Johnston. Sixth-graders listened with interest to stories about Anne Bradstreet, colonial poet, Phyllis Wheatley, first black poet in America, and Harriet Beecher Stowe. I also read to them about Elizabeth Blackwell, who became the first woman doctor in America. Many students were appalled that Elizabeth Blackwell was considered crazy and that some people thought they would be poisoned if they went to her.

Judith Viorst is a great favorite of my sixth-graders. We have read together, *The Tenth Good Thing about Barney*, *Alexander and the Terrible, Horrible, No Good, Very Bad Day*, and *My Mamma Says There Aren't Any Zombies, Ghosts, Vampires, Creatures, Demons, Monsters, Fiends, Goblins, or Things*. When I introduced the book *Free to Be . . . You and Me*, the first selection they wanted to hear was "The Southpaw" by Ms. Viorst. Other selections read from this collection were the poems, "My Dog Is a Plumber" by Dan Greenburg, "It's All Right to Cry" by Carol Hall, and "The Old Woman Who Lived in a Shoe" by Joyce Johnson. Throughout the remainder of the school year, I will be reading many of the other selections in *Free to Be . . . You and Me* as this book was high on the students' lists of favorites.

The last selection in the curriculum for this study was *William's Doll* by Charlotte Zolotow. This small book tells the tale of little William, whose father has supplied him with a basketball and a train, but in spite of these toys, he yearns for a doll. Why? Well, as the last pages reveal, he needs it so that he can practice being a father. I was surprised at the sixth-graders' acceptance of this book, so obviously contrary to anything they have experienced. None of my boys admitted to ever having wanted a doll, but they did say that they didn't think that dolls were all that bad for boys.

A few days after I had finished reading the books included in the study to the experimental group, I readministered the questionnaire to serve as a posttest. Results were tabulated, and the totals, shown in Table 2,

Table 2

Totals Selecting Each of the Three Responses—Posttest

Group	Bob	Jane	Either one
A	158	127	211
B	40	83	317
C	136	101	259
D	151	95	218

reveal the experimental group, Section B, produced an 81% increase in "either one" responses. The control groups combined produced an average 14% increase in "either one" responses.

An examination of the various item responses indicated that, in general, the items that showed the greatest number of "either one" responses were those items relating directly to curriculum material. The items concerning lawyers, surgeons, pilots, writers, veterinarians, judges, doctors, poets, and persons who work in office buildings all had 22 or more responses of "either one." All of these occupations were present in some detail in the books that were read to the experimental group. The items on the questionnaire registering the fewest number of "either one" responses were number three, concerning the role of secretary, and number nine, concerning the person who drives a dump truck. Neither of these occupations was read about in depth. Nowhere in any of the books was there depicted a male secretary, and only in *He Bear She Bear* was a woman portrayed driving a dump truck, obviously not enough to make an indelible impression.

One of the most perceptive questions asked by a student in the experimental group was, "Did mostly men or women write the books you are reading to us?" We quickly calculated the answer to this question and found that with the exception of Joe Lasker's *Mothers Can Do Anything*, Fred Phleger's *Ann Can Fly*, the husband-wife team of Stan and Jan Berenstain, and eleven contributors to *Free to Be . . . You and Me*, they were all women. It was noted that many of the illustrators were men, but the students suggested that more men should write books dealing with nontraditional feminine roles. Another student suggestion was that television begin to show boys performing more activities that traditionally have been considered feminine.

The past ten years have seen vast changes in the schools' educational programs, but educators must not rest on their laurels; there is still work to be done before children are "free to be . . . you and me."

References

Berenstain, Stanley, and Berenstain, Janice. *He Bear She Bear*. New York: Random House, 1974.

Clark, Linda. "Jack and Jill Fight Back." *Media and Methods* 12, no. 2 (October 1975): 22-27.

Georgeoff, Peter. "The Elementary Curriculum as a Factor in Racial Understanding." ERIC: ED 019 392, 1967.

Gezi, Kalil I., and Johnson, Barbara. "Enhancing Racial Attitudes Through the Study of Black Heritage." *Childhood Education* 46 (1970): 397-399.

Goldreich, Gloria, and Goldreich, Esther. *What Can She Be? A Lawyer*. New York: Lothrop, Lee, and Shepard, 1973.

—————. *What Can She Be? A Veterinarian*. New York: Lothrop, Lee, and Shepard, 1972.

Haller, Elizabeth S. *Images of Women: A Bibliography of Feminist Resources for Pennsylvania Schools*. Harrisburg: Pennsylvania Department of Education, 1973.

Hart, Carole; Pogrebin, Letty Cottin; Rodgers, Mary; and Thomas, Marlo, eds. *Free to Be . . . You and Me*. New York: McGraw-Hill Book Company, 1974.

Howe, Florence. "Sexual Stereotypes Start Early." *Saturday Review* 54 (1971): 76, 77, 80-82, 92-94.

Johnson, David W. "Freedom School Effectiveness: Changes in Attitudes of Negro Children," *The Journal of Applied Behavioral Science* 2 (1966): 325-330.

Johnston, Johanna. *Women Themselves*. New York: Dodd, Mead and Company, 1973.

Klein, Norma. *Girls Can Be Anything*. New York: E.P. Dutton and Co., 1973.

Lasker, Joe. *Mothers Can Do Anything*. Chicago: Albert Whitman and Company, 1972.

Litcher, John H., and Johnson, David W. "Changes in Attitudes Toward Negroes of White Elementary School Students After Use of Multiethnic Readers." *Journal of Educational Psychology* 60 (1969): 148-152.

Merriam, Eve. *Boys and Girls, Girls and Boys*. New York: Holt, Rinehart, and Winston, 1972.

—————. *Mommies at Work*. New York: Scholastic Book Service, 1973.

Phleger, Fred. *Ann Can Fly*. New York: Random House, 1959.

Roth, Rodney W. "The Effects of 'Black Studies' on Negro Fifth Grade Students." *Journal of Negro Education* 38 (1969): 435-9.

Sprung, Barbara. "An Overview of Non-Sexist Early Childhood Education." *Mediacenter* 1 (1975): 28-31.

Zolotow, Charlotte. *William's Doll*. New York: Harper and Row, Publishers, 1972.

Drawing Out Stereotypes

Sheryl Lee Hinman
Lombard Junior High School
Galesburg, Illinois

In a language activity lesson, junior-high students make discoveries about their perceptions and attitudes.

Before my students begin any discussion of religion, race, or sex-based prejudices, I try to make sure that they understand the definition of the word *stereotype*. To help students discover the meaning and development of stereotyping, I show them how obviously they have accepted oversimplified ways of judging groups of people.

I begin the class lesson by handing each class member four half-sheets of blank paper. I then ask students to draw, without looking at their neighbors' work, four different pictures—a teacher, a tourist, a dropout, and a mother. I suggest that they may want to label parts of their pictures. After students have had a chance to complete several of their drawings, I write the following definition on the board: A stereotype is a fixed idea about a group of people.

By comparing drawings in one class we noticed patterns emerging. There were many similarities in the teacher sketches. Eighteen out of twenty-two students had drawn women. Eleven of the pictures showed the teachers in obviously old-fashioned clothing. Thirteen of the teachers had unhappy or angry expressions on their faces. Students often added paddles, desks, or blackboards with math symbols or English grammar work. (In the three years I have used this lesson I have never seen students draw a gym, art or music teacher.) Quickly, students realize that they have pre-set views about whole groups of people.

Once the class understands the meaning of stereotype, there are several interesting questions a teacher may want to explore. For example, I ask, "Where do these impressions come from? How do we learn them?" Looking over their dropout pictures, many students mention that television commercials often portray people who leave school early as scruffy, unhappy drifters. The student drawings mirror the media image. Dropouts are generally dressed in old, tattered clothing; they have cigarettes, joints and motorcycles. The students also credit movies and television for producing the tourist stereotype. Almost every student draws an overweight man wearing a wild Hawaiian shirt and bermuda shorts. He carries one or more cameras.

Another interesting question is: Are the stereotypes good or bad? Of course, the bad attitudes held about teachers could hamper good relationships. But students were also able to mention several times when they thought the prejudgments were good. One student said, "Well, the scary picture of what happens to dropouts would certainly keep me in school. I don't want to end up that way."

One of the most controversial of the stereotype drawings is the mother. Most often students show the woman in a dress and apron. She is in the kitchen cooking or doing housework. More than half of the drawings show her as unhappy. I ask several questions about this drawing. Is it a true picture of the average mother? For instance, do they see their own mothers in dresses or slacks? How many of their mothers also have jobs? Again, I ask, "What are the sources of this stereotype?" Students sometimes recall old school textbooks that showed mother constantly cleaning or baking. Others mention advertisements. Next, we explore the question: If a stereotype is untrue, how might it be changed?

At the end of the class period, the student examples can be used further. I collect the drawings and put them up on the bulletin board. Across the top of the board I print the word STEREOTYPE followed by the definition. The class may want to bring in examples of stereotyping from current magazines, newspapers, etc.

The display can involve all students and reinforce their understanding of an important term. Students will freely compare their observations with the four stereotypes, and the discussion can prepare students for a more complex examination of the effects of many types of prejudice, including sex role stereotypes.

In Defense of Teaching the Concept of Grammatical Gender

Alleen Pace Nilsen
Arizona State University
Tempe, Arizona

*The writer describes word study activities which will help make children aware of the generic terms' potential for gender ambiguity.**

What can you as an elementary school teacher do to help children understand grammatical gender?

For one thing, whenever words come up such as *brotherhood, caveman, forefathers, mankind, man-made, chairman, spokesman,* etc., you can take the opportunity to explore the meanings with children. There are pressures being applied to get all of these words out of school materials, but it will be many years, if ever, before this is accomplished, so in the meantime take advantage of the opportunity to relate the study of language to a real communication problem.

If you are on a committee to screen books for sexist language, look a little deeper than the surface structure of sentences for sexism. I made a survey of several books that included generic terms in their titles and I found that the majority of them were indeed sexist both in what they talked about and who was pictured in the illustrations. But I did find an exceptional book of photographs entitled *The Color of Man* by Robert Cohen, photos by Ken Heyman (Random House, 1968), which included just as many pictures of females as males. This is an excellent book to use with children in helping them to learn the dual meaning of *man.*

One good activity is to take the list of generic terms given and, with students' help, put them in a timeline. Arrange them so that they show approximately when females started to be included in the meanings. For example, only men were literate during the middle ages, so at that time *penman* and *penmanship* referred specifically to males. In a similar fashion, only males received higher educations until just over a hundred years ago, so such common educational terms as *bachelor's degree, master's degree, fraternity, under* and *upperclassman,* and *freshman* were exclusively male terms. The timeline might extend into the future, comparing predictions about words depicting jobs where men almost

*This paper is a result of work done under a 1976 Arizona State University faculty research grant.

exclusively dominate (spaceman, garbageman, and milkman), with words depicting jobs where women are now also employed (policeman, mailman, newsman, etc.). This might also be a good time to look through a dictionary for "man" words. See how many of them are actually related to *man* meaning male and how many to other roots.

bachelor's degree	(to) master
baseman	master craftsman
bedfellow	masterful
brotherhood	masterliness
caveman	mastermind
chinaman	masterpiece
clansman	master's degree
committeeman	master stroke
common man	middle man
congressman	one-man show
countryman	patronize
craftmaster	penmanship
craftsman	salesmanship
craftsmanship	seamanlike
draftsman	seamanship
Dutchman	Scotsman
Englishman	self master
fellowman	showman
fellowship	showmanship
fellow traveler	spokesman
flagman	sportsman
forefather	sportsmanlike
fraternalism	sportsmanly
fraternize	sportsmanship
freeman	statesman
Frenchman	statesmanlike
freshman	statesmanship
gentleman's agreement	straightman
horsemanship	strawman
innerman	stuntman
Irishman	townsman
journeyman	tribesman
juryman	turkman
kingly	underclassman
kinsman	upperclassman
layman	(to) unman
manikin (mannequin)	weatherman
(to) man	whipping boy
manhours	white man's burden
man	wood craftsman
mankind	workmanlike
manpower	workmanship
manslaughter	workmen's compensation
marksmanship	yachtsmanship
master	yesman

Along with this activity, you and your class could make a collection of words that are, today, inexact descriptions of what they refer to. Many words of this type relate to technological developments in which language lags behind a new invention or process. Here are some of the words that my children and I have come up with, but give only one or two of these as examples and then, through discussion and observation, see how many your class can come up with.

> *Drug* stores sell more than drugs.
> Hair *permanents* last about three months.
> *Blackboards* are often green.
> Grownups are *kidnapped*.
> Airlines take *shipments*.
> *Teaspoons* are used for lots more than tea.
> There's hardly anything in a *dimestore* that costs a dime.
> I can have a *tea* without serving tea.
> *Glasses* are made of plastic.
> *Linens* are made of cotton.
> At *white sales* colored sheets and towels are sold.
> Eagles are called good *fishermen*.
> People talk about their dog's *personality*.

A related problem which commercial companies have is that their brand names become generic terms for a whole class of products, and then their advertising doesn't necessarily benefit them. Instead it benefits the whole group of products, which includes their competitors. For example, the Xerox company is presently fighting a campaign to keep their name from becoming the overall term for photocopying. Trade names that in the past have had this same trouble include *Coke*, which is used for any cola soft drink, *Kleenex*, which is used as a general term for facial tissues, and *fridge* (a shortened form of Frigidaire), which is used for any refrigerator.

The point of collecting examples of words that are currently changing meanings is to help children get a feel for the way language develops and for the fact that words cannot always be interpreted literally. Just as technology has brought new meanings to such phrases as "to *butter* (margarine) your bread," and "put the silverware (stainless steel) on the table," a changing culture has brought new meanings to many words which include a masculine marker.

It might also be interesting to look for words and phrases with a feminine marker which really apply to both sexes.I should imagine that black widow spiders and lady bugs, as well as sea cows, come in both male and female varieties. And it's interesting that domestic animals, which are important because of what the female produces, such as milk, eggs, or offspring, are more likely to be known by the female term than the male term. For example, *cow* is closer to a generic term than *bull*, *goose* is more generic than *gander*, and *duck* is more generic than *drake*.

One of the best activities to help a class or a small group understand and become aware of the problem is to make a collection of sentences from books, newspapers, magazines, songs, posters, etc., which include a word with *man* or one of its alternates in it. Through searching for contextual or pictorial clues, the students should be able to decide if the usage is intended to include (1) purely males, (2) females and males, (3) it's impossible to tell. A bulletin board with these three categories would be an interesting display. To get it started, you could bring in some sample sentences from such things as The Gettysburg Address, Bible verses, Christmas carols, and even the Declaration of Independence with its "All men are created equal."

This last example may lead into an interesting discussion of whether in 1776 women were excluded from full rights of citizenship in relation to the meaning of this word or simply from custom, i.e., were the authors making an explicit statement with their choice of wording? After all, the document did not start out with "All white men are created equal," but that was still the feeling and intent. Another interesting discussion might center around the emotional and psychological impact of being given an inaccurate label. A good word to use as a beginning for such a discussion is *babysitter*. By the time children come to school, they are no longer babies. Yet nearly all of them still have babysitters. How many of them have been bothered by the term? Should they be? What can they do about it?

Children, perhaps because they are so much closer in time to when they first learned language, seem to sense the miracle of language more than adults do. They have more fun inventing word games and secret codes. Perhaps students will enjoy inventing a new pronoun system and using it to rewrite a favorite story or news clipping.

The big thing is simply to make students aware of the problem. Their minds need to be trained so that whenever they come across a term that may be generic, a little caution light flashes in their brains and they are alerted to the need for figuring out the true intent of the writer or speaker.

People have voiced the opinion that by teaching children about generic terms, we are giving our approval and our blessing to sexist language. These critics feel that the long-range effect will be a general acceptance of generic terms with the masculine meaning. I disagree. I think that when children are made aware of the potential for ambiguity in such terms, they will be cognizant of the problem and will be on the lookout for ways of avoiding misunderstanding. When all of us—teachers and students— realize that the suggestions and the guidelines that are being offered have the simple goal of helping people avoid ambiguity, we will cease to feel threatened and will be able to put them to use in a natural—not a forced— way.

Women in Advertisements: Exploring Roles and Images

David A. England
West Virginia University
Morgantown, West Virginia

*Activities are suggested for sensitizing junior and
senior high school students to female sex
stereotyping in magazine advertising and enabling
them to analyze the selling techniques.*

*If there's anybody who really knows me, its Michael. He
says he loves the smell of my skin, and he likes my
perfume. . . .*

Presenting LONG JOHNS [cigarettes] for both sexes.

*We built this Cutless Supreme Brougham for Tom Richey,
a practical guy who likes to pamper his wife, Donna.*

*After 12 years at home, I started a new career. And I was
scared. I didn't think I would make it through my first
day. There were people I had never met whose names I had
to know; there was television equipment I'd never seen I
had to learn to use. What a day to try the anti-perspirant
test.*

The preceding "grabbers" from recent magazine advertisements illustrate a point that the NCTE Committee on Public Doublespeak has been
trying to make with English teachers: Advertisements can and do sell ideas
as well as products. Not surprisingly, new realizations about the role and
image of the American woman are reflected in virtually every magazine as
advertising agencies have been quick to capitalize on the American
woman's new self-awareness and more defined identities.

Using examples like the ones above makes it easy to interest junior and
senior high school students in devising strategies for analyzing female sex-
stereotyping in magazine advertising. The individual and group projects
described below prove to be as enjoyable as they are revealing. Most
interestingly, students are quite able to discover a type of ideological war
raging in American ads—a war of no small proportions between those
attempting to sell products to their ideal of the liberated woman, and those
who realize that not all women are, can, or even want to be liberated, and
base *their* appeals accordingly. As students monitored the ways in which
advertisers were riding the tide of social reform, they discovered *three*

categories of women "selling" products to their imagined counterparts in today's society: those appealing to the liberated woman, those appealing to the traditional woman, and those appealing to the woman in transition.

Students were easily able to understand the differences in appeals between Virginia Slims "You've come a long way baby" approach and that of a woman scrubbing floors with a smile because of Ajax cleaning power. The most interesting and subtly designed magazine advertisements, however, were aimed at women who wished to identify with both images— women who are assertive, but not too assertive, aware of their own identities but still pictured with a male, and superficially equal to men, while psychologically subservient. A woman pictured carrying a drink to a man after both had been remodeling a room is but one example.

The following activities, often designed by students and carried out by rather independent, self-sustaining groups of students, suggest possibilities which are enjoyable, informative, and pertinent.

1. Compare the way women are depicted in advertisements from several different magazines devoted specifically to male or female audiences. *Ms.* and *Playboy*, *Argosy* and *True Confessions*, and *Esquire* and *Cosmopolitan* will provide interesting contrasts. Students conducting such investigations have discovered a logical consistency between a magazine's projected readership and ways females are depicted.

2. Look for examples of a reaction against women's liberation as the main basis of appeal, i.e., the anti-Virginia Slims philosophy: "Make things a little easier for your wife, a woman proud to admit her place is still in the home." With this as a starting point, one group began looking for other reactionary plays in magazine advertisements—ads for example, which pushed consumerism in an ecologically aware time, or cigarette smoking in spite of the surgeon general's warnings.

3. Create original ads for the same product but written for the three types of women currently being appealed to by contemporary advertisements. Demonstrate how language, pictures, and underlying ideologies would be manipulated to make the same product appeal to the different types of women. In this activity, students created magazine ads for household cleansers, purchased by the liberated woman, but used by the man of the house, and ads for colognes to make women more successful in the business world, etc.

4. Collect and analyze a variety of samples illustrating how stereotypes of traditional women are used in advertisements and how the women's liberation movement has been exploited by advertisers. Why, for example, was a woman *school teacher* chosen to make a pitch for BankAmericard, students asked. The roles of liberated women being projected by advertisers

fell into major categories—the now woman in the business world, the sports world, and just quite independently "doing her (variety) of things."

5. Suppose an alien from another planet had only magazine advertisements to use as a basis for generalizations about women in contemporary society. What would be some of the conclusions reached? One group of students theorized that, if a certain group of ads were chosen, women would be viewed as a group of slaves to a larger, more powerful, and more intelligent population. Still another group found magazine ads which, in isolation, would convince an alien that this planet was designed for, and dominated by, a sort of super, queen-like species—the woman.

6. Write a satire based upon some of the conclusions reached above. Once concepts of how women are depicted were understood by the class, this became a popular and productive project. A particularly clever group of sophomores wrote a two-act play dramatizing how a group of aliens might report back to their superiors—basing their generalizations on how women were depicted in movie magazines.

7. Explain how women are used to sell products to men. What is revealed about the advertiser's conception of the contemporary woman? In cases where men are used to sell products to women ("Even at a costume ball, remember underneath it all . . . gentlemen prefer Hanes") what is revealed about male attitudes toward women? High school boys were particularly impressed with the important new realization that the way a woman's role is perceived by a man determines how the man tests the woman. For example, one project was based on male–female roles and interaction as the sexes were depicted in magazine automobile ads.

8. Analyze issues from the same magazine over the last ten-year period in order to assess how the ways in which women are pictured in ads have changed. Magazines like *Time* and *Newsweek*, since they reach both male and female audiences, will point to certain conclusions about how Madison Avenue's conception of the contemporary woman has (in some cases) changed.

9. Analyze how particular industries (automobile and tobacco particularly) use men and women to advertise products. What are the implications of the varied ways in which men and women make their appeals? What assumptions can be made about men (and women) on the basis of how men and women sell the same product? Students were intrigued by conclusions such as (1) women seldom sell nonfiltered cigarettes and (2) when women "sell" liquor, ads usually show them with a mixed drink, more often than not with a fruit (or very sweet) flavor.

10. Suppose women suddenly appeared in advertisements for products traditionally sold exclusively by and to men. What are the potentials for satire?

11. Consider certain "syndromes" that have been created in the last few years as a result of women's changing roles. Students found over a dozen different products being sold in magazine advertisements showing women on the tennis court. Billie Jean King as a type of "model woman" and the development of women with "macho" characteristics (a lot of leather clothes, riding horses, driving jeeps) were phenomena discovered by students.

12. Design and implement an "action program" in which demeaning or stereotyped roles of women in magazine ads are protested to the proper agencies. One entire class worked most of a semester in documenting their cases and appealing to local advertisers, television stations, product manufacturers, advertising agencies, and government bureaus.

13. Collect data and draw some inferences about the physical character-istics of women in magazine advertisements. Students drew some revealing conclusions after they found that the women depicted were blonde, tall, ideally proportioned, smiling, and immaculately groomed far more often than they found in their own observations. Interesting, too, was a relationship discovered (and documented) between a woman's image and her height—the more liberated women were pictured as being *taller* than their over-bound counterparts.

14. Consider the future of the woman's role and image in advertising. If current trends continue, how will women be pictured in the magazine advertisement of 1995?

Capitalizing on the availability of magazine advertisements as a basis for the study of sex-role stereotyping in the media provided starting points for many other related projects. Abilities to analyze, document, report, and to think creatively were increased. The end result was that students realized how the desire to be associated with a particular type or group can be a powerful inducement to buy certain products. High school students are interested in actively exploring the selling of ideas—and they become more intelligent, socially aware, and articulate consumers in the process.

Think It, Feel It, Be It: Nonsexist Experiences for the Classroom

Marilou R. Sorenson
Margo Sorgman
University of Utah
Salt Lake City, Utah

A series of exercises was tried in the classroom to modify the sexist perceptions and, at the same time, to strengthen the self-concept of both male and female children. These exercises can be adapted to all levels.

Children develop their sex-role identity from the expectations of the "significant others" in their lives (family, friends), the institutions in which they spend most of their formative years (schools, religious groups, clubs), and the media which occupy more and more of their leisure time (television, radio). Traditionally, these identities have been limited by rigid sex-role concepts. However, we are becoming more acceptant of the androgynous personality which combines both masculine and feminine characteristics. To assist teachers in modifying stereotypic thinking by strengthening the self-concept of both females and males, we have developed a number of nongraded exercises for use in the classroom.

Each of these activities has been tried with students and the appropriate modifications made. Teachers have indicated that they were helpful in generating discussions about the social roles assigned to men and women. The average length of each activity is thirty minutes and the materials needed in each activity are listed with references for commercial resources.

What's in a Name?

Brainstorm a list of streets, buildings, sports teams, hurricanes, schools, cities, cars, companies, rivers, ships, etc. Code these for male/female/animal. Discuss the attributes which probably resulted in the naming. (Example: stormy, unpredictable behavior may have resulted in female names for hurricanes).

Who Can I Turn To?

List ten of the most important people in your life. Code the list using the following categories: family, friends, male, female. Which ones would you go to to solve a problem, to make a pie, to build a table, to learn to ski, to do your homework, to attend a hockey game/symphony? Discuss whether the listing falls into gender categories.

Mothers and Others

1. Bring in an assorted collection of pictures of women. Have the students categorize those pictures into mothers and nonmothers. Use the following questions for discussion: Which ones are mothers? What other things do women do? Do you know any women who are _____ (ex.: doctors)? Is it possible for a woman to be a _____ (ex.: doctor)? Is there anything a woman could not be? Of all the things you could be, which three would you most like to be? Would you hire a female _____ (ex.: principal)?

Then show pictures of famous mothers. Discuss their ability to be both professional women and mothers.

2. Have students make a booklet of "Mother" words, mottoes, proverbs, colloquialisms. Examples: Mother's Day, mother's helper, Mamma's boy, mother lode. Have the students keep adding to the listing.

3. Have students write poems about their mothers. Discuss the poems using these questions: What was the mother doing? What words were used to describe her? List and compare the activities and descriptions for sex-role stereotyping. Then read and discuss *Thanks, Mom* by Susan Polis Schutz (*I Want to Laugh, I Want to Cry*. Boulder: Blue Mountain Arts, Inc. 1973).

> Since I had a mother
> whose many interests
> kept her excited and occupied,
>
> Since I had a mother
> who interacted with so many people
> that she had a real feeling for the world,
>
> Since I had a mother
> who was always strong
> through any period of suffering,
>
> Since I had a mother
> who was a complete person
> I always had a model
> to look up to
> and that made it easier
> for me to develop into
> an independent woman.

Extended Activity. These activities can be rewritten for fathers.

Make it Work

1. Give students a listing of professional occupations such as news-

caster, tennis champion, president of a country, member of Congress, mayor of city, movie star, scientist, writer. Have students indicate whether this position would be filled by a male or female. Then bring in pictures of famous men and women in these positions. Have students continue building up the collection for a bulletin board entitled, "Who's Who in the News?" Have a display of books and pictures showing people in various roles (for example, Irwin Stambler, *Women in Sports*, Doubleday & Co., 1975).

Extended Activity. Have the children fill in work role inventory by matching the person with the job. Discuss which roles were typically female, male, or open to both.

Role	Man	Woman	Both
doctor			

Other occupations: teacher, cook, police officer, lawyer, principal, engineer, chemist, television star, dentist, parent, pilot, babysitter, pharmacist, college professor, writer, president of corporation, artist, dancer, nurse, firefighter, carpenter, plumber, salesperson, athlete, musician, politician.

2. Compare the role of women in various times through the use of children's literature. For example, Louisa May Alcott's *Little Women* (Grosset & Dunlap, 1868) and *A Wrinkle in Time*, Madeline L'Engles (Farrar, 1962). Some discussion questions might be: What were the opportunities for women? How did women spend their time? List three advantages/disadvantages women had in each time period. Which time period would you rather live in?

3. Simulation game called "Pick the Candidate." Give children descriptions of four candidates for a job. Example: 22 years old, female, Caucasian, college graduate, loves children, worked in summer camp, tennis champion; 22 years old, male, Oriental, college graduate, worked in day care center, on football team. The job might be physical education teacher in elementary school. Divide the class into small groups and have them decide which candidate they would hire. Discuss their choices with questions such as: Which qualities helped the candidate? Which did not? What kind of person were you looking for? Did age, sex, race effect your choice?

4. Invite resource people who have chosen nontraditional occupations to your classroom: male nurse, female dentist. Interview each person with the following questions: Why did you choose this career? What barriers have you confronted in the career? What has been most difficult about the job you now hold? What do you like best about your job? How did your family/friends feel about your choice? If you had it to do over, would you choose the same position?

Extended Activity. Have a display of pictures of men and women in nontraditional occupations. Prepared sets can be obtained from Professional Women and Community Helpers, Feminist Resources for Equal Education, P.O. Box 3185, Saxonville Station, Framingham, Mass. 01701. $2.50 ea. set.

5. Have each student list (or draw) each member of the family (him/herself included). List three things each person likes and dislikes to do. Discuss why certain tasks are performed by certain members of the family. Then have students fill in "Who Does What Inventory."

Task	Mother	Father	You	Brother	Sister
grocery shopping					

Other tasks: uses tools, does laundry, uses sewing machine, plays baseball, cleans house, washes the car, does the dishes, talks on telephone, plays with dolls, does gardening, watches television, plans summer vacations, goes to work, gets car fixed, pays bills, invites people to house, buys presents, reads newspaper, buys most of books. Discuss listing to determine if these tasks are tied to sex-role stereotypes.

Fabulous Fantasies

Have students read or recall some fairy tales. Use trait list inventory to analyze stereotyping.
Trait list:

Trait	Male	Female
wise		

Other traits: responsible, ambitious, lazy, important, kind, cruel, strong, active, loving, giving, selfish, calm, violent, intelligent, stupid, brave, cowardly, dependable, gentle, creative, destructive, obedient, curious, foolish, weak, inactive, unloving, excitable, harsh.

Discuss the results with the following questions: Was the main character male/female? How many male characters/female characters were in the story? Who was the good person or force in story? Who was the evil person in the story? Who created the problem? Who solved the problem? Who needed help? How do you feel about the story?

Extended Activity. Have students rewrite the fairy-tale for nonsexist characterizations. Using the trait list and questionnaire, analyze TV programs, cartoons, commercials and other advertisements. Have students rewrite some of them.

Subtracting Adages

Give students some stereotypic adages such as: "Father knows best," "Only sissies cry," "Boys shouldn't play with dolls," "Woman's place is in the home!" Have students brainstorm others. Select one adage and role play a situation.

Extended Activity. List TV programs that follow the theme of the adage.

Trying on New Behaviors

1. Bring to class a collection of "typical" toys (perhaps three for males, and three for females). Have each student select four from the collection that they would like to receive as gifts. Discuss choices that were most popular. Of the four, which would you give to a girl? Which would you give to a boy? Which were never chosen and which were always given to boys/girls?

Extended Activity. As a group, design a nonsexist toy. Discuss purpose, color, function, design, etc.

2. Role play the following situations: Billy wants a dress for Halloween, but his friends laugh at him. John wants a doll and his family react to his choice. Betty wants a pair of boxing gloves and her girlfriends make comments about this idea. After the role playing discuss the activity. Could this happen? Why would it happen? Has anything like this happened to you?

3. Suggested nonsexist titles for reading and discussion:

> Cleaver, Vera and Bill, *Where the Lilies Bloom*. Lippincott, 1969.
> Fitzhugh, Louise, *Nobody's Family is Going to Change*. Farrar, 1975.
> Hirsch, S. Carl, *He and She*. Lippincott, 1975.
> Klein, Norma, *Girls Can Be Anything*. E. P. Dutton, 1973.
> L'Engle, Madeline, *A Wrinkle in Time*. Farrar, 1962.
> Merriam, Eve, *Boys and Girls, Girls and Boys*. Holt Owlet, 1972.
> O'Brien, Robert, *Z for Zachariah*. Atheneum, 1975.
> O'Dell, Scott, *Island of the Blue Dolphins*. Houghton Mifflin, 1960.
> Radau, Elaine, *Hidden Heroines in American History*. Messner. Photos, 1975.
> Sabin, Francene, *Women Who Win*. Random. Photos, 1975.
> Skorpen, Liesel M., *Mandy's Grandmother*. Dial, 1974.
> Surowiecki, Sandra and Lenthall, Patricia, *Joshua's Day*. Lollipop Power, 1972.
> Waber, Bernard, *Ira Sleeps Over*. Houghton-Mifflin, 1972.
> Wolde, Gunilla, *Tommy Goes to the Doctor* and *Tommy and Sarah Dress Up*. Houghton-Mifflin, 1972.
> Zolotow, Charlotte, *William's Doll*. Harper and Row, 1972.

Neuter Genders

Read a story without using names and pronouns. Have students complete the characterization. Sample themes could be: breaking a window, baking a pie, becoming President of the U.S., killing an animal, making a flower arrangement. Discuss why they assigned the genders they did to the characters. Read some actual stories which depict characters in these situations in nonsexist roles.

Seeking Insights

Helping students to recognize sexism provides a strong base for the more important and more difficult task of promoting understanding. Why is it important to study sexism? Who is hurt by the restrictions of an ingrained sexist philosophy? How can we change our habit of stereotyping others? Seeking Insights *offers a variety of approaches to these questions with a group of exercises adaptable to all grade levels.*

Flannelboard Families Have Flexible Roles

Carole Schulte Johnson
Inga Kromann Kelly
Washington State University
Pullman, Washington

Children developed enlightened ideas about sex roles in a first-grade unit about families.

Background

The stereotype of the nuclear family with its rigid sex roles is established early in the socialization process. Several teachers in our school were concerned with the self-concept of children whose families did not match the societal "norm," as well as with the attitudes of others toward such children. We felt it was important for children to recognize the validity of a variety of family patterns, as well as to understand that factors other than sex are important in determining what "jobs" family members have within the family structure. These "jobs," or task roles, whether undertaken by children or adults, tend to serve as models for future behavior.

This project was a component of a first-grade unit on The Family, but would also be useful in a study of Career Awareness.* It incorporates many language arts skills, such as listening, vocabulary and concept development, oral expression, discussion skills, critical thinking, and problem-solving. It can be adapted to any level from preschool through grade three. Our format encompassed five sessions of twenty to thirty minutes each; however, procedures can be modified so that several family patterns are presented and discussed in a single, extended session.

Pupil Objectives

1. To gain experience in problem-solving.
2. To acquire a realistic view of the variety of family patterns in our society.
3. To recognize that many tasks need to be done to keep the family unit operating smoothly.
4. To recognize that every family member can assume some responsibility for carrying out defined tasks.

---

*We wish to acknowledge the contribution of students Vickie Schmitz and Kristi Watson through their pilot project in this area.

5. To understand that the roles family members assume in carrying out needed tasks are determined by factors other than sex. Factors include what needs to be done, demands on other family members in and out of the home, age and size of family members, and individual preferences.

Materials

1. Flannelboard, approximately 30" x 36".
2. Cut-outs of family members such as father, mother, male and female children of different ages, possibly grandparents and other relatives. Cut-outs should be 6½" to 7" high for adults, proportionately shorter for children.
3. Job cards approximately 3" high, and of sufficient length for a word, phrase, or picture to identify jobs such as cooking, sewing, mowing the lawn, earning money, etc. Teacher prepares cards in anticipation of jobs which pupils will identify. Blank cards and felt pen should be available to add other jobs as suggested during discussion. A long card with caption "Boys and Girls Do All Kinds of Jobs" is needed for final session. Figures and cards should be backed with felt, pellon or similar material which adheres to flannel.
4. Chart paper for recording family and job information from one session for use in subsequent session.

Procedures

Four different family patterns are presented on four successive sessions with the fifth session being used for summarizing and generalizations. Possible family patterns are:

1. Father, grade-school age son, preschool daughter
2. Father, fifth-grade twins, boy and girl (Alternative: mother instead of father)
3. Father, mother, grade-school age son, preschool daughter
4. Father, mother, junior high school son, first-grade daughter

Combinations or modifications of the above families can be used. The following procedures are simply illustrative; teachers are urged to adapt, modify, or expand as appropriate to student level and sophistication.

Session 1

Teacher arranges board so everyone can see. While this project can be used with entire class, more meaningful involvement is likely if group can be kept at ten to fifteen children. Prepared job cards should be near teacher so she/he can readily see and reach them. The following dialogue is for illustrative purposes only.

Teacher: "Today we're going to talk about families and some of the jobs that need to be done in a family. What are some of these jobs?" (As children name jobs, teacher places job card on flannel-board.)

Suggested discussion questions:

1. What needs to be done when people in the family get hungry?
2. Does anyone have a cat or dog? What needs to be done if you have a pet in the family?
3. What needs to be done when your clothes get dirty or torn?
4. What jobs might a family need to do outside the house?

When the concept of "jobs" is well established, the teacher points out that there are many jobs that need to be done in a family. This list of tasks on the job cards can be reviewed briefly to reinforce the concepts of family and jobs.

Teacher: "Now we're going to look at one family. In this family there is a father, (place cut-out figures on flannelboard as they are introduced), a son who is in fourth grade, and a daughter who isn't in school yet. Let's see who might do the jobs that need to be done in this family.

"How do you think this family gets money for food and clothing?" (Father probably has a job.) "With father working and the son in school, what do you think happens to the daughter?" (Perhaps she goes to a day care center, or a sitter comes in, or a neighbor or relative cares for her.) "Now let's look at the jobs we said needed to be done. Let's think of who might do this job." (Pick one of the cards on flannelboard.) "Let's put the card under the person who would do it." (Children identify person to do job and place job card in appropriate place.)

When all jobs have been assigned, teacher and pupils look over the board. If any jobs have been mis-assigned, such as preschool daughter doing the sewing, they can be discussed at this point, with teacher guidance in assessing who can best do the job and why.

Teacher: "Who seems to have the most jobs in this family? Yes, it looks as if father does. Do you think he's going to be able to do all this and be at work all day, too? What might he do?" (We got a quick response that he can get married and mom can do the jobs!) "Who else might help?" (Son might help after school.) "Are there any jobs that a four-year-old could do?"

Discussion is carried as far as appropriate to meet objectives. To summarize, the teacher says, "Today we learned about one kind of family. Who was in this family? How did we decide who did which job? Are all families like this one? Next time we will look at a different family and see how they might get jobs done." When session is over, the teacher makes a quick felt pen sketch on chart paper of family members and respective jobs to compare with new family in subsequent session.

Session 2

The teacher brings out flannelboard from Session 1, showing family members and jobs assigned to each.

Teacher: "Who were the members of our first family? How did we decide who would do which jobs? Today we have a different family. Here is the father, but now we have a son and a daughter who are twins in the fifth grade. Let's look at our jobs. Do you see anything that might be different?" (Remove previous family members and replace with new family.)

Suggested discussion questions:

1. Who might do the cooking? Do you think father, son and daughter could take turns? Why could the daughter help in this family when she didn't cook in the last family?
2. Who could do the dishes? Can boys and men do dishes just as well as women and girls?
3. Who might mow the lawn and shovel the snow? Can girls do these jobs?
4. What kind of sewing might need to be done in this family? Who might do it?

Children should be encouraged to talk about jobs their own family members do or might do. The teacher can stimulate new ways of looking at work by relating own experiences, such as, "When I was in fifth grade, my younger brother and I took turns doing dishes," or "When I was little, my older brother showed me how to use a sewing machine."

Teacher: "Suppose that instead of twins, the boy is in high school. Do you think any of the jobs might change?"

To further reinforce the concept that task performance is not necessarily determined by sex, the teacher can make a change as follows:

Teacher: "Let's suppose this family is just a bit different. Instead of the father, let's say that the family has a mother. (Make change on flannelboard.) Now, we have a mother and two children. The mother has a full-time job outside the home. What changes do you think there will be in the jobs?"

Presumably, the children will generalize that the mother will do the jobs previously assigned to the father, and that tasks thus are assigned on the basis of factors other than sex.

Teacher: "Let's look at the chart of our first family. What is different about the way jobs are done in our second family?" (Family members share or rotate more jobs when children are older.) "Does it make a difference in jobs whether the grown-up in the family is the mother or the father? Why not?"

Session 3

After a brief review of previous families and jobs, the teacher introduces a new family.

Teacher: "Today we have a family with a mother, a father, a son in the third grade, and a daughter who is two years old. Let's think about jobs in this family. What are some things we need to know before we can decide who might do which job?" (Who earns the money in the family?) "Suppose the father works to earn the money and mother stays home. Who might do which jobs now?" (Results may show that mother ends up with almost all of the jobs.) "Why does mother have so many jobs? Might there be too many jobs for one person even if that person doesn't work outside the home?"

Suggested discussion questions:

1. Suppose father becomes ill and isn't able to work for some time. What changes might need to be made in the family? (Mother may get a job to earn money.) How might the jobs at home change?

2. Suppose the mother and father both have jobs outside the home. Who takes care of the daughter? What changes might we make on our job chart?

3. Suppose both mother and father work outside the home, but the girl and boy are both in junior high school. How might the jobs change?

4. Suppose mother and father both work; both children are boys in junior high school. Does this change what jobs family members do?

Teacher: "Today we had both mother and father in the families. Did mother and father have the same jobs in each family? Why did the different families have different people doing the jobs? Was it important whether a boy or a girl did the job? What changes were there when both parents worked outside the home?"

Session 4

Teacher presents a family with a father who works outside the home, a junior high school son, a first grade daughter, and a mother who is a college student.

Suggested discussion questions:

1. What might be different in a family when mother goes to college? (She has to have time to study and to go to class. Her schedule isn't the same every day. There may need to be greater flexibility in home jobs, such as when she has a term paper due or has a big test.)
2. I know a family where the father does most of the cooking and the mother does the yard work. Why do you suppose that is? (Introduce idea of individual preference.)
3. What if a person gets tired of doing the same job all the time? Can family members trade jobs? What about jobs nobody wants?
4. What if the son doesn't like to do the laundry? Is it important for boys as well as girls to know how to do laundry?
5. How can jobs be assigned according to what one likes best to do? How can a family make sure that jobs are given fairly?

Session 5

All job cards are removed from flannelboard. Teacher holds up card labeled "Earn Money."

Teacher: "Who in a family could earn the money?" (If only father is named, ask who else might earn money.) Hold up another card such as "Make Beds." "Who could do this job? Who else could do it?" (As children respond, teacher guides with questions such as, "What would happen if this child were older or younger? What if this person doesn't like that job? What if both parents work?") Arrive at generalization that many factors such as age, other responsibilities, individual preference, etc. affect who does what job.

"Now let's think about the jobs in our own school and classroom." (Use heavy string to divide flannelboard into two columns. Place cut-out of boy above one column and girl above other column.) "What are some jobs that need to be done in our room?" (Have children list jobs such as cleaning boards, taking play equipment out, watering plants, taking milk count, etc.)

"Let's look at our flannelboard. Who can do each of these

jobs? Which jobs do you like best?'' (Read list of jobs and have children raise hand for their preferences.)

"We see that boys and girls like many different jobs." (Remove string divider and place caption "Boys and Girls Can Do All Kinds of Jobs" across board.) "What does this card say? What does it mean?"

Follow-Up

After the formal lessons, the teacher may use many opportunities to review and reinforce the ideas, referring often to the flannelboard family. Children can make up their own families and arrange job cards as an independent language arts activity.

Reactions to the five sessions as well as to the follow-up activities were highly positive. To insure a successful experience, teachers should be aware of some precautions which came to our attention during the course of the project:

1. Avoid drawn-out sessions. When a point seems clear, move on to the next one.

2. Involve children by having them place figures and cards on flannelboard as often as possible, in addition to encouraging discussion.

3. Avoid making value judgments about sex-typed jobs when children share own family experiences. When a child says, "Oh, my father never washes dishes," or "My father says that's woman's work," the teacher can respond with comments such as, "But I'll bet he could wash dishes if they needed to be done," or "Yes, people used to think that some work was only done by women and some only by men." It is important that the child be spared the impression that his or her parents' views are "bad."

Feminist English Teacher vs. Holly Dalton, Student Nurse

Linda Kennedy Floyd
John Marshall High School
Rochester, New York

Girls read "boys' books" and boys read "girls' books" in a project that led junior high school students to examine and study sex-role stereotyping.

My early attempts to raise the consciousness level of my eighth graders were soundly thwarted, enough so that had I not been convinced of the need to foster an awareness of sexism, I would certainly have abandoned what seemed to be a futile crusade. For as surely as I would appear one morning with an armload of materials and ideas for consideration (more often for *ridicule*, if not total disregard, from both sexes) so would I find myself at the end of a frustrating day contemplating a swift return to *Warriner's* and safe, if antiquated, territory. Finally, happily even, something worked!

Prompted by heated controversy over the upcoming state ERA vote, there was an increase in debates, impromptu discussions, and question and answer sessions in classes. In order to clarify issues and to provide a forum for opinions and questions, I encouraged open and honest (frequently distorted and even abusive) exchanges in the hope that eventually they would become aware of sex discrimination as it exists in real life and in literature. Much of the information I had provided them regarding sex-role stereotyping had gone way over their heads or had been thoroughly rejected because it was "unnatural," so I went in search of something with which they could more realistically identify.

As a follow-up to these discussions, I made a reading assignment. I asked students to select individual books of fiction with two specifications: (1) the protagonist(s) should be a teenager; and (2) the choice of book should reflect the opposite of their usual selection (i.e., girls would read books with male protagonists and vice versa). At first, there were moans of protest and mumbled oaths about me and my "lib" ideas. (I was obviously a libber, wasn't I? Didn't I use Ms. instead of Mrs.? Well . . . ?) What impressed me most initially, though, was the ease with which the girls accepted the assignment in contrast to the anguish exhibited by boys who browsed through titles ranging from something like *Holly Dalton, Student Nurse* to *Seashore Summer*, muttering what I suspected to be obscenities peppered generously with my name. (Were the girls exhibiting the passivity I expected? Or were they anxious to try a "boys' book" out of curiosity? And were the guys threatened by having to read a "girls' book" and to risk menacing epithets from their peers?) A few boys searched for books without jackets which announced the subject in graphics with over-sized lettering, while the girls went to the charge-out desk with their selections entitled *Chuck Foster, Camp Counselor* and *Treasure on Misty Mountain* as if the assignment were either routine or actually unique.

To facilitate careful scrutiny of fictional characterization and an accurate and fair assessment of situations in their books, I provided students with scorecard sheets (sample shown) to use in gathering data and assessing their characters. These sheets were to be used for an immediate accumulation of information, i.e., first impressions as to depiction, dialogue, action, characteristics of protagonists. The exercise was a practical method of helping students size up images and portrayals, to understand stereotyping in literature, and to begin to grasp an under-standing of what sexism is and where it exists in their own lives—at home, at school, at play. It's one thing for me to advocate change in the library and to recommend nonsexist reading selections. It's quite another to teach students self-reliance in making judgments and decisions based upon their own sensitivity to sexism in literature and their lives.

The reading project utilized books already in the library, thereby avoiding an expenditure which might be hastily and poorly planned due to the nature of the project. It proved to be highly successful as an end in itself, though it was intended to be a means to an end, that end being a lively group discussion/exchange of books, characters, readers' attitudes, assessments, and comments. Some students' inhibitions were overcome and even some of the most reluctant participants took an active part in the discussions. Students became less and less defensive about traditional roles for characters, recognizing that males and females alike are limited when they are cast in roles dictated by society. Although most boys were initially convinced that there were "men's jobs" and "women's work," and that no *real* woman, for instance, should play football or drive a truck or fight in the armed forces (the three most often suggested examples of what women's libbers *really* want, of course!), many changed their minds and expressed amazingly liberated points of view, giving sound evidence of astute observations. The girls who had passively accepted the assignment in the beginning were given to animated participation in discussions, even chancing alienating their peers. The seminar was both an eye-opener and a consciousness-raiser!

It also lent itself to other areas of study. Writing, for example, could easily be generated from discussions, and students might share private thoughts, values, or ideas about sexism with their journals, if not with other students and teacher. Role-free stories were another possibility. Media study (examining sexism in television and movies), language study using both student language and textbok language, and creative dramatics, a veritable treasure-trove for role-playing situations and a vehicle for speaking and listening exercises in evaluating sex roles, were three additional areas of study. Finally, and just as importantly, I reinforced my contention that adults have no monopoly on allegiance to and perpetuation of tradition. Even the most inexperienced, the coolest, the most naive eighth grader comes to me bound up in a sex role, most certainly limited and resistant to change. Compared to the senior high student, however, the eighth grader will be easier to reach, to touch, to teach.

SCORECARD SHEET FOR INDIVIDUAL READING

Fiction/Teenage Protagonist
Title _____   Author _____

Circle the appropriate responses and/or write in your own responses:
1. The main character in my book is   (a) male   (b) female.
2. Another major character is   (a) male   (b) female.
3. The male characters are   (a) interesting   (b) not interesting   (c) both.
4. The female characters are   (a) interesting   (b) not interesting   (c) both.
5. The things that the males do are   (a) interesting   (b) dull.
6. The things that the females do are   (a) interesting   (b) dull.
7. The experiences/adventures/jobs that males have are   (a) exciting   (b) dull.
8. The experiences/adventures/jobs that the females have are
                                          (a) exciting   (b) dull.
9. List the major characters, their sex, and occupations/jobs:

Character	Sex	Occupation
_____	M F	_____
_____	M F	_____
_____	M F	_____

10. I like _____ because _____
            (character)

11. I dislike _____ because _____
            (character)

12. The males in the book are   (a) active   (b) passive.
13. The females in the book are   (a) active   (b) passive.
14. The conversations/dialogue of the males is   (a) interesting   (b) dull.
15. The conversations/dialogue of the females is   (a) interesting   (b) dull.
16. This is a   (a) girl's book   (b) boy's book   because_____

Expanding Horizons with Poetry by Ear and by Eye

Karla F. C. Holloway
Michigan State University
East Lansing, Michigan

At Clinton Junior High School in Buffalo, New York, the author used poetry by black women writers to help pupils discover the false picture that racist and sexist stereotypes paint of black females.

In many language arts curriculums today, one can find some recognition of the existence of the black writer, who has again "come into vogue," to use Langston Hughes' Harlem Renaissance pronouncement. Unfortunately, and predictably, in this still inadequate treatment of an important aspect of American literature, black female writers are not given the attention their considerable achievements have earned for them.

American society has assigned stereotypes to black women because of their race and their sex. These stereotypes victimize not only black women but also nonblacks, male and female, whose critical faculties and intellectual development are stunted by their acceptance of the false pictures that stereotypes project. The classroom teacher has no more important task than that of liberating young minds from the shackles imposed by the ignorance and prejudice that stereotypes foster.

As a black woman English teacher, one way that I undertook that task with my eighth-grade students was to acquaint them with the point of view of black women as seen through the mirror of their literature. For my unit, I decided to use poetry and to include contemporary as well as earlier writers. Narrowing this group to just six poets, I chose one poem each by Gwendolyn Brooks, Jessie Fauset, Margaret Walker, Frances Harper, Margaret Danner, and Lucille Clifton.

The criteria for selection of the poems to use with my lively adolescents had to be established carefully. I decided that the poems should be short enough for oral lessons, and except for Margaret Walker's "For My People," which I would not miss including, I was able to find suitable short pieces. I wanted to give the children experience with free verse and a variety of rhyme schemes and rhythmic patterns. Mood and tone needed to vary among these pieces to keep the attention of the children.

The occurrence of poetic devices that were easily identifiable by this age group was a consideration in selecting the poems. One of the side benefits of using early black writers was the lesson in dialectal varieties of English from another time. Poems fitting these criteria, and at the same time portraying girls and women, or lending themselves to the formulation of opinions about the woman author's personality and point of view, were easy to find.

In each case the children's first task was to read the poem silently, and then reread it, this time underlining their favorite parts. In this way, the "instruments" of poetry were often picked out by the students themselves. The ensuing "I underlined this word or that phrase because _____" session often resulted in a free-wheeling discussion that was filled with valuable insights.

After listening to me read the poem aloud, the class read aloud with me. Usually, on first trial the lack of unity in cadence and intonation in the students' reading blurred the effectiveness of the poem and gave us the perfect occasion for discussing the meaning and importance of tone. Sometimes I asked such questions as, "Why is it important that we know how a poem feels in order to read it well aloud?" or "How can we say this line in a way that expresses excitement (or sorrow, fear, confidence, etc.)?" "What does the adverb do to the adjective in a line like 'We real cool'?" "How can we express that idea orally as a class?"

"We Real Cool" was the Gwendolyn Brooks poem that I selected. Using a tape recorder and constant playback kept each student alert as we practiced the lines and discussed what we could do to translate the effect of the written word into oral expression. The result with Miss Brooks' poem was a reading beginning with a soft yet forceful articulation of the first lines, and a gradual crescendo to an explosion of volume with the final line: "We/die soon!"

Eventually the male students, in exaggeratedly deepened voices, took over the line. The result was a complete oral success and a clear understanding of the nature of the woman who could write with compassion and clarity of vision about seven boys in a pool hall.

Jessie Fauset's poem on Sojourner Truth, "Oriflamme," was a favorite. The girls recorded their own creative interpretation of the first verse, capturing the anguish of the symbolic black mother whose leadership, they reasoned, was inspiring, never overbearing or domineering. They liked knowing that they were giving full meaning to the strange-sounding word "reft." The last verse belonged to the boys, who spoke as Sojourner's "myriad sons," "fighting with faces set."

Because of its length, I had the class select, after the first reading, parts from Margaret Walker's "For My People" that were most impressive for recording and perfecting. A thoughtful discussion led them to choose the first verse, the third verse ("playmates" and the enumeration of so many familiar play roles caught their attention at once), the fifth verse ("For the boys and girls"), and the last verse, on which they loosed great fervor in a ringing determination. Some students added a percussion background, using their desks as drums to beat out the irresistible rhythms. Antiphonal readings helped students delineate the many changes of persona within a poem. The children added spirituals, street sounds, and church service chants as background for the reader's imaginative interpretations of the deluge of sights and sound in the poem. "For My People" was a perfect vehicle for reinforcing a realistic, unbiased image of the black woman.

The same kinds of opportunities for understanding change of person, tone, and mood in the oral reading and for understanding the perceptions and emotions of a black woman were there for us to discover in the other poems. Frances E.W. Harper's "The Slave Auction" moved the children into an experience few of them had ever imagined. "Sadie's Playhouse" by Margaret Danner linked the past with a present as real as the wallpaper described in the poem, wallpaper which the children might see at home every day. Although there were as many interpretations of "My Mama Moved Among the Days" as there were children in the class, something about this short poem by Lucille Clifton appealed to them. Everyone underlined "like a dreamwalker" and "right back on in."

This was a unit in which each student added an important dimension to the whole class's study and appreciation of poetry. At the same time, the poetry of these black women revealed to the children the many faces of black women, faces that showed such qualities as love, perseverence under pressure, gentle grace, joy in the celebration of goodness, rejection of evil and injustice, and pride in family and race. No stereotypes emerged. Instead, the students realized that here were human beings to be understood.

Children who have studied, understood, and enjoyed the works of black women writers are less likely to accept as true a stereotype of a black woman that a dominant and domineering culture has defined and would foist upon them. Like my own class, if given the opportunity, children everywhere will appreciate the artistry of black women writers and can learn many valuable lessons from the ability of these writers to deal with any subject and every concern with depth and perception.

Role Models:
Cultural vs. Literary Definitions

Arlene Reva Honig Pincus
Pearl River Middle School
Pearl River, New York

In teaching her eighth-grade class to examine stereotyped views, the author used a novel about an adolescent girl along with the students' descriptions of what they imaged as a day in their lives as adults.

I have long believed that literature provides role models for children, that sexist and racist books teach and reinforce sexist and racist beliefs, and that, if the hidden curriculum of literature is the curriculum of stereotyping, teachers who fail to challenge that curriculum are themselves the teachers of stereotypes. It was these convictions which led to an investigation of what kinds of stereotypes my students believe about men and women and what kinds of self-stereotyping they do.

One thing I wanted to know was what kinds of possibilities my eighth graders envision for themselves as adults. Therefore, I asked them to describe an ordinary day in their adult lives, and then I charted both the boys and the girls according to the careers they imagined for themselves.

Boys:		*Girls:*	
Policeman	4	Teacher	9
Pro Football Player	4	Interior Decorator	3½
Doctor	3	Nurse	3
Lawyer	3	Stewardess	3
Auto Mechanic	3	Secretary	2
Pro Soccer Player	2	Beautician	2
Veterinarian	2	Nursing Home Worker	1
Pilot	2	Dog Breeder	1
Construction Worker	2	Lawyer	1
Electrician	2	Optician	1
Architect	2	Policewoman	1
Welder	1	Ambassador	1
Marine Scientist	1	Veterinary Assistant	1
Lineman	1	Housewife	1
Pro Basketball Star	1	Actress	1
Company President	1	Receptionist	1
Computer Technician	1	Virologist	1
Bank President	1	Motorcycle Shop Owner	1
Garbage Collector	1	Reporter	1

Teacher	1	Day Care Center Worker	1
Forester	1	(part time)	
Formica Cabinet Maker	1	Fashion Designer	1
Ship's Captain	1	Veterinarian	1
Boatyard Owner	1	Violin Teacher	½
Pro Hockey Player	1	Undecided	1
President of Lincoln-Mercury	1		
Unemployed	1		

Because almost all the students named careers, at first glance this chart might leave a less stereotyped impression than is accurate. Further analysis led to the conclusion that the girls made choices of careers that were both lower paying and less physical than the choices made by the boys. In addition, most of those boys who named nonprofessional careers could not reasonably expect to qualify for professional job training on the basis of their school performance at the time of the survey. This was not true of the girls who named housewife, secretary, or part-time day care worker; all these girls had the ability, based on their school performance at the time of the survey, to go to college and succeed there.

The students' actual descriptions of their imaginary days differed even more according to sex. The boys described a typical day in their adult lives largely by reporting what went on on the job while girls usually recounted a juggling of their work time and their family responsibilities. For example, one boy wrote:

> "I woke up in the morning and got dressed. Then I jogged around the park for about half an hour. Then I went back to the house, I washed up and I had breakfast. Then I walked down into town to my office. My secretary told me that a Mr. Blue was waiting in my office . . . I walked in and he wanted to get right down to work. He asked me if I would design a very special building for him. I told him some of my plans and he agreed completely. . . . "

Another boy who aspires to be an electrician wrote:

> "I got up at eight and got dressed, then went to work. I went to check one job to see if they were doing it right. I got a call that someone was hurt at another job. The man had been trapped under a pipe so I called an emergency crew to help him. . . . "

Still another boy's essay read:

> ". . . I had tons of work to do, as usual. I had to review planning charts and floor plans for some new houses. . . . I had a late lunch appointment with a big client. I wondered if I should bring the contract along. I decided to bring it since it would be better to have it if he wanted to sign. This guy really had me worried. If I lost him my Boss would kill me. . . . "

Almost none of the boys included families in their imaginary day; the few who did included them only marginally:

> "I get up out of bed at 8:00. I go to breakfast, talk to my wife, and then drive to work...."

> "5:30 PM—went home to tell my family the good news...." (a patrolman who has just captured a robber)

In marked contrast, the girls almost always described a typical day as being centered around home and family. Some typical responses were:

> "7:00—wake up and feed kids and get them off to school
> "8:00—get washed and dressed
> "8:30—get houswork done
> "9:30—go down to studio....
> "11:45—begin shooting film....
> "3:00—call babysitter to pick up kids from school...."
> (an actress)

> "Monday, 8:00. My alarm radio went off. I get up to prepare the baby's food. Wake up my husband and my two boys. Fix their breakfast, then the baby wakes up. Feed her and get the rest off to school and work. Put the baby to bed. Get dressed. By then it is 10:00. I wait for ... the babysitter. Then I get my car out and go to my law office. My job is from 10:30 to 4:30 unless I am in court. I get to my client and we prepare our case. At 4:30 I leave and pick the boys up from school and drop one off for football practice...."

> "I wake up at 8:00. I get dressed then, have a good breakfast. I do my exercises. I wake up my husband so he can get up and go to work. My children have already gotten up and left for school.... I prepare breakfast for my husband...." (a teacher)

Very few of the girls neglected to mention whether they had families. One atypical response read like this:

> "I have been working as a clothes designer for five years. I usually get up at 8 and I get to my office around 9:30. I start the day by looking over what I designed the day before...."

Another unusual essay began:

> "As I crawled out of bed at 6:00 ready for a new day I thought of the beautiful day it was and how bad it must be to have to be in bed everyday. I ... laughed at the thought of Mrs. Reddings mixing her tomato juice with orange juice. I hurried through breakfast and shower and was gone by 7:30...." (a nursing home worker)

Even though a few essays did not follow the usual pattern, it was clear that most boys were already thinking more about jobs than family, and most girls plainly considered family more important than job. Given this situation, I thought it very important to introduce some novels about adolescents who do not express stereotyped world views. I hoped that by doing this, I could provide my students with some possibilities in life they might not have otherwise considered for themselves or others.

Of course, it is almost impossible to find a novel about an adolescent girl who isn't fat, pregnant, psychotic, or on drugs. Many novels are too openly sexual to be permitted in an eighth-grade classroom. There were no such problems with books about boys. There is an abundance of contemporary novels in which adolescent boys deal with real problems, face moral dilemmas, and make decisions. I searched for such a book about a girl for several months.

When I first read *Never Jam Today* by Carole Bolton, this historical novel about a young suffragist in 1917 did not appear to meet my needs. It was too corny, I thought during the initial reading. Mental images of my thirteen-year-old students responding to dialogue like, "Oh dear! . . . This is no way to act at dinner. We'll all have indigestion. Let's change the subject. . . ." [1] held me back even as my political side drew me to the book. Look at all the issues it raises, I argued with myself. What could be a better parallel than the New York women winning a state amendment on women's suffrage in a year when the state Equal Rights Amendment is to come before New York's voters? What better way to teach about the conflicts between militant politics and pacifist sentiments that raged throughout this country not only during World War I but during my students' early years? What a perfect way to ask why every eighth-grader has heard of Tom Paine but not Abigail Adams, of Jefferson and Lincoln, but not Sojourner Truth, of Henry David Thoreau and Martin Luther King, but not Elizabeth Cady Stanton or Alice Paul or Carrie Chapman Catt.

In the end, though, it was not history or politics which made me decide to teach *Never Jam Today* to a class of eighth-graders still high on empathy for John and Lorraine of Paul Zindel's novel *The Pigman*. Rather, I decided to use the book despite its flaws because the protagonist, Madeline Franklin, has a feminist consciousness believable for 1917, and because this protagonist has a chance to marry either of two men—Matt, who respects her head, but doesn't turn her on, or Jamie, who turns her on, but doesn't respect her head. Madeline chooses to marry neither of them. Instead, she decides to move out of her parents' home and make her own way in the world. The last page of the book reads:

> " . . . She thought of her friend, moving into her Brooklyn apartment tonight. Rosemary had broken free from her past. Could she, Maddy, do it too?
>
> "Again she could hear Rosemary's wistful voice saying, 'I'll have to

---

[1] Carole Bolton, *Never Jam Today* (New York: Atheneum, 1971), p. 13.

find someone to share it with me. . . . '

"After all, Maddy had some money saved. . . . In a pinch, Aunt Augusta would lend her anything she really needed until she finished college and got a full-time job.

"Thinking of that, Maddy opened her closet and dragged out a small suitcase.

"When she came down the stairs . . . the lion emerged . . . nodding at the suitcase. 'Good! I see you're going to stay [overnight] at your aunt's.'

" . . . 'No,' she said.

" . . . 'I remembered I had an appointment somewhere else. There's a note on my dresser, Papa.'

"She edged toward the front door as her perplexed parent asked, 'An appointment? Where?'

"Maddy swung open the door and leaped out. 'In Brooklyn !' she called back ecstatically, and she ran down the front steps."[2]

It seemed reasonable to me that even if students were only considering very traditional work and marriage models for themselves, they would at least be able to understand and appreciate that a character like Madeline Franklin would choose a different sort of life. To test this out, I concluded a rather lengthy reading guide, intended to help explore literal, interpretative, and applied levels of the reading, with what I considered a relatively easy applied question:

"It is ten years since women got the vote. Pretend you are Aunt Augusta, writing to your old friend, Mrs. Armbruster. Tell her what has happened to Maddy in these past ten years. Make sure you reveal in your letter that Maddy could have chosen to marry Matt, or Jamie, or even Bud Harris. Instead, your niece went to live with her friend Rosemary and attended college. Include all the important things that have happened to Maddy since she made that decision. Make sure you reveal your personal feelings about Maddy's choice!"

I speculated that students would imagine that Maddy did indeed go to college and get a job, but I also thought that they would have Aunt Augusta express disapproval for Maddy's decision, both because there is some justification in the book for believing that Aunt Augusta would have liked Maddy to marry Matt, and because I expected the students themselves to disapprove of Madeline's decision.

The actual responses of my students differed significantly from my prediction, as can be seen in the tabulated results.

The range of answers proved that the students harbored a variety of views on the way things should turn out. Some students seemed to ignore the book's ending by marrying Maddy off to one of her boyfriends; others put her through school only to marry someone else, or to settle into a

---

[2]Ibid., pp. 239-240.

secretarial or teaching position. Those who were willing to cope with the book's ending either disapproved ("I should never have got her mixed up in suffrage"), thoroughly approved ("Maddy's whole perspective on life has changed tremendously. . . . Maddy makes up her mind about things and has her own opinion about things"), or were ambivalent. These latter papers were produced by very mature and intelligent girls. One of the most articulate writers wrote:

> "My most rebellious young niece, Maddy . . . . is doing just fine for a working girl. . . . Little did I know when I introduced her to suffrage she would become such a changed person. Suffrage has not only changed her political life, but also her social life. Even after the amendment passed, she has continued to rebel against normal standards for a woman. Maddy has had three proposals of marriage. She has refused them all! . . . . She said she needed to be free. . . . after she refused Jamie's proposal she went and moved in with a young girl she knows from work. Yes, she certainly is free. Maybe yet she'll settle down. Maddy has a good job as a secretary and is looking for a job. . . . [which will let her use] her four years of college. . . . She has so many boyfriends; not one is serious though. Her parents have seemed to accept her now. . . . the other young girl moved out and got married. I think that set Maddy restless and regretful. Maybe something will happen soon. . . . "

Clearly, students took very different ideas away from the same experience.

The person who probably learned the most from *Never Jam Today* was me. My original assumption, that literature provides people with possibilities in life that they may not otherwise consider for themselves or

Conclusion	Percent of Boys (n=27)	Percent of Girls (n=31)	Percent of Total (n=58)
1. reverses ending	25.9	16.1	20.7
2. acknowledges ending but changes focus so that marriage is of primary importance.	22.2	29.0	25.9
3. acknowledges ending but expands in a stereotyped way	11.1	0	5.2
4. acknowledges ending but fails to expand	14.8	0	7.0
5. acknowledges but disapproves of ending	7.4	19.4	13.8
6. acknowledges ending but expresses ambivalence	0	16.1	8.6
7. confirms and approves of ending	18.5	19.4	19.0

others, has been modified to include the notion that there are some possibilities people are incapable of considering, however innocuous those possibilities may seem to me.

The message of *Never Jam Today* was not that marriage is wrong for all people in general nor that it was wrong for Madeline specifically, but rather that marriage could not and would not be the most important thing in Madeline's life. That so many students failed to absorb that message was not a failure of reading comprehension in the simple sense, but rather an inability to believe and apply a message which conflicted with students' assumptions about what should be important to a seventeen-year-old girl.

Although more and more nonsexist curricular materials and books are being written and purchased, these materials, and teachers who understand and approve of them, are going to have little effect on students when the message from the larger society is not simply that they are wrong, but that they are unthinkable. American kids are brought up to devote themselves to jobs and families if they are boys, and families and maybe jobs if they are girls. Teachers and materials which say a woman's life can legitimately be devoted to ideas may well remain in a holding pattern until the larger society catches up.

Chicana Literature and Sex-Role Stereotyping

Carlota Cardenas de Dwyer
University of Texas at Austin
Austin, Texas

Through reading and analyzing certain Chicana poems, secondary students are encouraged to acknowledge and appreciate cultural diversity in attitudes toward identity and stereotyping.

Just as current reassessment of the American national character can provide the basis for meaningful examination of the many distinct "American" cultures and the role each plays in a particular literary work, so may concentrated focus on the cultural identity of some women authors yield valuable insights into the role and dynamics of ethnic components in "women's literature." Whereas all females in the United States have been subsumed, by implication anyway, under such encompassing labels as "the woman's point of view," or "women's rights," it is important to note that the ratio of the American ethnic majority and the various American minority groups remains constant, in spite of the fact that the factor of gender has been eliminated from consideration. Eighty-seven percent of women are white women; black women, Chicanas, and other groups still represent a statistical minority. Most significantly, the automatic imposition of such inclusive phrases as "sexual stereotyping" fails to acknowledge the generations of cultural diversity which distinguish one group from another. Because of the ineradicable effects of history and tradition on a writer or group of writers, one should approach all works with a willingness to discover differences and similarities between groups and among individual artists.

To illustrate the great variety of images Chicana women have of themselves and of some of their common experiences, it is not necessary to peruse all of the literature recently published by American women of Mexican ancestry. A representative selection is offered in a 1975 text available from the University of California, Irvine. *First Chicano Literary Prize*, a collection of prize-winning short stories and poetry by nineteen Chicano authors, contains a number of fine selections which verify the scope and skill of both Chicano and Chicana writers. However, it is in the works of a single Chicana writer that readers might be introduced to the special images some Chicana writers have of themselves.

Rita Mendoza significantly begins her collection of eighteen poems, "Thoughts of a Chicana Woman," by unequivocally projecting her ethnicity as a more critical distinguishing characteristic than her sexual identity. In "I'm a Chicana," the speaker rejects invitations to pass as Anglo, French, or Spanish. The poem concludes with her unwavering, "I'm a Chicana," and a slight note of irony.

I'm a Chicana

You could pass for an Anglo, they tell me if you tried,
I said "I'm a Chicana," my head bent-down—I cried.
You could pass for a French girl, they tell me if you tried.
I said "I'm a Chicana," eyes downcast—tried to hide.
You could pass for a Spanish girl, they tell me if you tried,
I said "I'm a Chicana," eyes straight-ahead, sad, dried.
You could pass for a Chicana, no one has ever tried.
I said "Thank you," my head held up with pride.

RITA URIAS MENDOZA

Discussion Questions:

1. What are some of the implications of the phrase "to pass for"?

Possible Response: While some students may be able to point quickly to the obvious, external act of public disguise, others may extend the point further and question the possibility of eventual self-deception or rejection.

2. How do the three proffered alternative identities, Anglo, French, and Spanish, relate to each other and, in contrast, to the speaker's own choice, Chicana?

Possible Response: Students may simply consider the three terms as random non-Chicano possibilities. It might be brought out also that the three are European or Caucasian types, and an essential part of the Chicano/a racial heritage is nonwhite, i.e., Indian.

3. In separating herself from the "they" of the poem, the speaker clearly establishes discrete social units. Who are "they"? Does the speaker necessarily stand alone?

Possible Responses: Non-Chicanos are placed at a distance, but the speaker need not be considered an *isolato*; other Chicanas might share her perspective and feelings.

In contrast to "I'm a Chicana," Chicano men as well as women are represented in Mendoza's next poem, "Rape Report," because here the author uses sexual assault figuratively to denote the violation of a language. While the poem might be most appropriately considered as an imaginative exercise in extended metaphor, rather than as an example of belles lettres, it nonetheless dramatizes the interplay of ethnic and sexual issues in the poet's mind.

Rape Report

He pushed me down and tried to force me to give in.
When I told him he couldn't have what was mine,
   he used strong-arm tactics on me.
I fought back, I clawed and screamed
   and for fighting for my honor,
I was punished even more.
He said, "I am doing you a favor, if you
   submit, it will be easier on you."
I knew I was losing ground and then knew
   it would be less painful for me if I quit fighting.
He received praise for what he did to me.
He took something that was sacred and beautiful
   to me and replaced it with four-letter words.
I am making this report in English, you see,
   I've been raped of my native tongue.

RITA URIAS MENDOZA

Discussion Questions:

1. How specifically can you identify the two personalities in this poem? To what or whom does the "he" of the poem refer?

Possible Response: The brutalizing force of the poem is probably Anglo America. Although the loss of the speaker's "native tongue" is specifically lamented, the entire culture of a whole people might be included. (Some students may reject the notion of such blanket indictments, discounting it as a form of generalization itself.)

2. How are the male and female roles presented? Does each have a recognizable character?

Possible Response: Students will probably agree that the author reveals conventional sex-role stereotyping in her presentation of the male factor as aggressive, violent, and destructive.

Although Mendoza uses rape metaphorically in "Rape Report," it is the actual reality she writes about in "The Rapist." The "he" clearly refers to the arrogant perpetrator, while the writer identifies herself with all outraged women and speaks of a united group in phrases like "after we destroy him." Details of ethnicity do not seem to have any mention or relevance in this poem. While the poet embraces all womanhood in her use of "we," it is interesting to note that the females characterized here are not the intimidated victims of "Rape Report." They are aggressive, vengeful, even slightly sadistic!

The Rapist

There's a rapist loose in town
    trying to pull our panties down
Twelve attempts, and 3 completed
    Is that a terrific fete?
He'll get his we'll see to that
    when we chop off his bumbling bat
After we destroy him,
    we'll laugh, we'll jeer
Bastard, can you hear?

RITA URIAS MENDOZA

Discussion Questions:

1. How is society divided in this poem? To whom does the "we" refer?

Possible Responses: Students will observe no distinctions here, except sexual ones. The "we" appears to include all women.

2. What kinds of qualities and feelings are ascribed to women in relation to a rapist?

Possible Responses: Retaliatory and vindictive feelings emerge.

As just these three poems by Rita Mendoza indicate, great variety in sex-role stereotyping, as well as in images of self, is discernible in the works of

Chicana writers. This variety is not unrelated to the boundless contrasting, sometimes contradicting, concepts generated by other American writers. Whatever the content may be, it is crucial to develop the critical skills necessary to recognize, and eventually to reconcile, the different approaches with the myriad variegations of the American character itself. In conclusion, students might investigate some of the ethnic or multi-ethnic anthologies now available for more examples of writing by women of other minority groups.

Supplementary Activities

1. Exposition. In a short essay compare and/or contrast the work(s) of two women writers, focusing primarily on their self-image and evidences of sex-role stereotyping.

2. Persuasion. In an essay of prescribed length support or refute the following thesis statement: American women of diverse ethnic backgrounds share more similarities than they do differences.

3. Interviews. Compose a series of questions regarding the thesis given above and interview some of your classmates, male and female, about their feelings on this issue. Report back to the class.

References

Cardenas de Dwyer, Carlota, ed. *Chicano Voices*. Boston: Houghton Mifflin, 1975. An anthology of contemporary Chicano literature by and about women, with a section on the Chicana woman. Instructor's guide available.

Gonzales, Sylvia Alicia. *La Chicana Piensa: The Social-Cultural Conscious of a Mexican American Woman*, 1974. A bilingual collection of prose and poetry available from the author at the English Department, San Jose State University, San Jose, California 95192.

Ortego, Philip D., ed. *We Are Chicanos: An Anthology of Mexican American Literature*. New York: Washington Square Press (Pocket Books), 1973. An extensive and well-balanced gathering of literature, including several female authors.

Portillo, Estela, ed. *Chicana Literature*. El Grito Book Series. Berkeley: Quinto Sol Publications, P.O. Box 9275, Berkeley, California 94709.

Strategies for Exploring Sex-Role Expectations through Literature

Barbara Stanford
Utica College of Syracuse University
Utica, New York

Several approaches to reading and discussing literature help high school students sort notions about sexual identity in the effort to understand their own sex roles.

Perhaps twenty years ago students didn't need help understanding the difference between masculinity and femininity. Sex roles were more clearly defined then—when a man wouldn't be caught dead crying or wearing cologne or working as a telephone operator, or when a woman knew that her place was in the home and left the wearing of pants to her husband.

But now we're investigating whether males are innately more aggressive than females or whether they've just been conditioned by social forces to act that way. We're finding out that there is no inherent reason why men should do the heavy manual labor while women tend the children; some societies are managing quite nicely with a very different division of labor. We're seeing American women demanding not only equal pay for equal work, but a host of other rights, including the right to open doors for themselves, ask men for dates, and decide whether they want to have babies. And, perhaps in reaction, we are seeing the beginning of a men's liberation movement, seeking for men the freedom to be passive as well as active, to show emotions, and to be totally ignorant of how to change a tire.

This welter of changing and often conflicting views of the proper role of a male or a female makes it very difficult for students to come to terms with their own sexual identity. Since so many of the works of literature read in the English class deal either directly or indirectly with issues of sexual identity, reading and discussing literature is a natural vehicle for helping students sort through the many notions about sexual identity and come to a satisfactory understanding of their own sex role.

One approach is to deal with possible sex-role stereotyping in the novels the class is reading. Have each student choose a novel to read independently or have the entire class read the same novel. Then give the following homework assignment:

Examine your book very carefully—page by page if necessary—to discover differences between male characters and female characters in the way they act, the things they talk about, the extent to which they express emotions, and the attitudes of others toward them. Also consider the following:
  a. Who takes the lead in making decisions (e.g., where to go on dates)?
  b. Who calls whom on the telephone?
  c. Who seems to be the most intelligent? the most sensitive? the most "emotional"?
  d. Who protects the other from "danger"?
  e. Who seems to have the most interesting plans for the future?
  f. Who exhibits the most socially undesirable behavior?

After students have made their lists, divide the class into small groups of approximately five students each and have them share their answers to the following questions:

  a. Describe how men and women differed in your book.
  b. Does your book seem to stereotype men and women? (If you don't understand what stereotyping is, find out.)
  c. Do you feel that the book(s) your group has read contains more or less sex stereotyping than movies or television?
  d. Do you *like* the way men and women are portrayed in the books you read?

Another approach is to prepare several descriptions of characters excerpted from works of literature, giving options for all personal pronouns so that the reader does not know for sure which sex the character is (see the examples below). Read each excerpt aloud—or better yet, give each student a copy—and ask the class to guess which excerpts describe males and which describe females. Don't tell them the title of the books from which they came; this often gives away the answer. Discuss the following questions:

  a. What clues suggested to you the sex of the character?
  b. How accurate were your guesses?
  c. Do you think that the author exaggerated sexual characteristics or are men and women really that different?

Here are some excerpts that are appropriate for this activity. Find similar excerpts in other books you are familiar with or which you want to encourage students to read.

EXCERPT A: Sayward the oldest, went back to the haunch over the fire, turning it on the hook catching some of the dripping in a long whittled spoon and basting it with its own juices. *He/she* hadn't given away to *his/her* feelings since *his/her* small hand had guided *his/her* younger brother into the world.

(from *The Trees* by Conrad Richter)

EXCERPT B: *Johnny/Janie* Blakeworthy was burned by the suns of Africa to a dark brown, and *his/her* eyes, in a dried wrinkled face were grey, the whites much inflamed by the glare . . . . *He/She* was thin: *he/she* spoke of having had malaria recently. *He/She* was old; it was not only the sun that had so deeply lined *his/her* face. In *his/her* blanketroll *he/she* had, as well as the inevitable frying pan, an enamel one-pint saucepan, a pound of tea, some dried milk, and a change of clothing. . . . .
(from "The Story of a Non-Marrying Man" from *The Temptation of Jack Orkney and Other Stories* by Doris Lessing)

EXCERPT C: One of these fools was my *Aunt Kristin/Uncle Konrad*. Not that *he/she* was less bright than my father or any other villager. Quite the contrary. *He/She* was sly enough, driven by an ambitious spirit that the others might well have envied. Yet nothing went right for *him/her*. To *his/her* credit, *he/she* did not hang *his/her* head or become despondent over *his/her* failures: instead *he/she* renewed *his/her* efforts and even displayed a remarkable awareness of the tragi-comical aspects of all *his/her* endeavors.

(from *Peter Camenzind* by Herman Hesse)

You might also pass out copies of a page reproduced from the catalog of a publisher of paperback books, the order sheets for any teenage book club, or a list of the books your English Department requires or recommends students read. Ask each student to list three books that he/she would like to read and three books that she/he definitely would not like to read. Have the class tabulate the number of males who wanted to read each book, the number of females who wanted to read it, the number of males who did not want to read it, and the number of females who did not want to read it. Then discuss the following questions:

 a. Which books did the two sexes respond to differently?
 b. What characteristics of books do males seem to like that females do not?
 c. What characteristics do females like that males do not?
 d. Do the books usually taught in English classes appeal more to boys or girls? If there seems to be a bias one way or the other, what possible explanation can you give?
 e. What kinds of books do males and females like equally?

Still another approach is to have students read novels about the destructive effects of exaggerated sex-role images on the lives of people. Many well-known novels portray males and females fighting against restrictive sex-role images or giving in to the restrictions. Examples that come to mind immediately are *Madame Bovary, Far from the Madding Crowd, The Bell Jar, The Cheerleader, Trying Hard to Hear You* and *Sticks and Stones*—all of which are available in paperback. Even if each student reads a different book, the class could come together for a total-group discussion of the following questions:

a. What traits generally accepted by society as being appropriate to his/her sex did the main character in your book possess?
b. Demonstrate visually in a collage, a diagram or a drawing the qualities that the main character in the book possessed. Then show with either a second drawing or collage or a superimposed diagram the limitations that society tried to put on the character.
c. What happened to the character in your novel? What do you think would have happened if the character had been accepted completely as he or she was?

Mythology opens the door to discussion of sex roles. The myths of almost every culture include stories that attempt to define ideal maleness and femaleness. We are the heirs of many of these images and we are still shaped by them in many ways. You might wish to begin by explaining to the class that most primitive people personified the things and events around them and told stories about them. As these things and events came alive in stories, they usually became either male or female. Ask students to consider the following list and to imagine that they were creating a mythology. Ask: "Which of these would you turn into males and which into females?"

love	the ocean
war	corn
fertility	the largest river near your home
sun	earth
moon	thunder
peace	fire
home	wisdom

Tabulate on the board the responses of all class members. Note which items were usually seen as male, which were usually seen as female, and which were sometimes seen as one and sometimes as the other. Ask students to speculate on the reasons for these results. Then introduce students to the Greek gods (with a book such as *Heroes, Gods and Monsters of the Greek Myths* by Bernard Evalin). Note which gods and goddesses were associated with each natural phenomenon. Determine the Greeks' associations with each natural phenomenon and compare their perceptions with those of the class.

Assign students to investigate the mythologies of various other cultures (using a book such as *Myths and Modern Man* by Barbara Stanford) to determine which natural phenomena were portrayed as male and as female by these groups. Discuss the following questions:

a. Based on the evidence you have obtained from the myths, does there seem to be a universal concept of maleness and femaleness?
b. What qualities, if any, appear to be universally associated with males? with females? What qualities are seen as male in some cultures and female in others?

c. Do the myths of our own culture influence our ideas today? Would our ideas of maleness and femaleness be different if we had grown up with a culture based on American Indian myths, for example?

For additional activities of this type, see *Roles and Relationships: A Practical Guide to Teaching About Masculinity and Femininity* by Gene Stanford and Barbara Stanford (New York: Learning Ventures/Bantam Books, 1976), from which the activities in this article were adapted.

Analyzing Sex and Gender

Ellen D. Kolba
Montclair, New Jersey

In a word analysis lesson, high school students can explore the role that language plays in shaping their perceptions.

An exploration of language and its relationship to the real world can be very revealing. It need not be technical, for students can easily see that one way of finding out what ideas we have about words (and thus about the world) is to chart this unconscious knowledge in some way.

The assumptions we make about sex and gender lend themselves well to feature analysis. In one or two lessons that can be followed up in a variety of ways, students can begin to distinguish between the gender and what we assign as the sex of a noun.* Discovering why it is necessary to mark gender in a different way from sex will also enable students to verbalize what they may know unconsciously about our difference in meaning for words like *woman*, which is marked for sex, and words like *surgeon*, which is marked for gender.

You can begin the lesson by presenting students with a series of sentences like these:

1. (a) She hurt himself.
   (b) Give this coffee to my mother. He likes it with milk and sugar.
   (c) My brother Andrew prefers hers with sugar only.

---

*I am indebted to Mary Ritchie Key for this distinction between sex and gender, which she makes in *Male/Female Language* (Metuchen, N.J.: The Scarecrow Press, 1975).

Discuss what is wrong with these sentences. Students should see that each one contains a noun (or in the case of (a), a subject pronoun) that is very clearly either male or female, and that as a result, there is a lack of agreement between these nouns and the pronouns referring to them. These sentences are ungrammatical. They violate a rule of grammar that requires a pronoun to have the same features as (or agree with) its referent.

Next, present a series of sentences like these:

2. (a) He is vivacious.
   (b) Uncle Howard had a baby.
   (c) Her aggressive tactics were much admired.

Ask students whether these sentences sound as wrong as those in the first group. Ask, too, whether there is any grammatical rule involved here, such as the rule of pronoun agreement in the first group of sentences.

Students should see, for the second group of sentences, that the problem is not in the form of the words (e.g., whether *him*self or *her*self should be used), but in the attributes we attach to certain words. For example, *vivacious* strikes us as descriptive only of women, and so it jars us when it is linked to a subject that is clearly male.

For both groups 1 and 2, encourage students to add examples of their own. In group 1, all the sentences should exhibit violations of grammatical rules. In group 2, all the violations should be semantic—violations of our assumptions about the *meaning* of words.

When students have finished making additions to these two lists, ask them to look at the referents in the sentences they have written. Are they all clearly male or female—words like *he, she, sister, brother, aunt,* and *uncle*? If some sentences have less definite referents, words like *actor, author, cousin, teacher,* ask students to put these into a separate group for now. Then present them with a third list of examples:

3. (a) The surgeon put on her mask.
   (b) The babysitter raised his voice.
   (c) The manager held herself accountable for every mistake made in the department.

This time, ask students to compare these sentences with the sentences in group 1. They should see that the issue in these sentences, as in group 1, is the grammatical relationship between a noun and a pronoun referring to it. Then ask whether any of the group 3 sentences is ungrammatical in the way that the group 1 sentences are. Although some of the sentences may seem odd to some students, emphasize the fact that there is no lack of *grammatical* agreement between *surgeon* and *her* or *babysitter* and *his*. Neither noun is clearly male or female, though our knowledge of the world we live in may incline us to think of one as male and the other as female. To reinforce this point, have students try these sentences:

4. (a) The surgeon put on his mask.
   (b) The babysitter raised her voice.
   (c) The manager held himself accountable for every mistake made in the department.

Point out that, grammatically, these sentences and their counterparts in group 3 are equally valid. Unless we know that the specific surgeon referred to is a woman or a man, either *his* or *her* will agree with the noun.

Finally, discuss with students a set of sentences like these:

5. (a) The surgeon is vivacious.
   (b) That actor is beautiful.
   (c) The manager had a baby.

Comparison with group 2 should show that these two groups of sentences are alike in the problems they may create. The semantic relationship between the words, not the grammatical one, is at issue. Words like *vivacious* and *beautiful* may have feminine connotations for us, just as words like *actor* and *surgeon* may have masculine connotations. Unlike the sentences in group 2, however, the gender of the subjects in group 5 is ambiguous—these nouns are not clearly either male or female, despite their connotations. And so the semantic discrepancy in these sentences is not as great as in group 2. Both *The surgeon is vivacious* and *The surgeon is handsome* are acceptable.

Once students have distinguished between grammatical and semantic features, they can take a closer look at how grammatical features are marked and, in the process, discover the distinction speakers of English make between sex and gender.

Have the students return to the sentences in groups 1 and 3 and examine them side by side:

1. (a) She hurt himself.

   (b) Give this coffee to my mother. He likes it with milk and sugar.

   (c) My brother Andrew prefers hers with sugar only.

3. (a) The surgeon put on her mask.

   (b) The babysitter raised his voice.

   (c) The manager held herself accountable for every mistake in the department.

Help students to see that each sentence contains a pronoun (*himself, her, his,* etc.) that indicates a specific sex or gender.

Now have students look at the words these pronouns refer to. Point out that if we wanted to show all the things included in our understanding of a word, we could make a list of the characteristics, or features, of the word. For example, *mother* could indicate several underlying characteristics—animate, human, female, etc. All of these words contribute to our understanding of how it is used. By making such a list, we are also showing that the opposite of each of these features—inanimate, nonhuman, male—does *not* characterize this word. We are showing that the word can occur in certain kinds of grammatical relationships (Mother sang to herself; Mother liked her own room best), but not in others (*Mother sang to himself; Mother liked its own room best*).

Continue by asking students whether each of the pronoun referents in groups 1 and 3 has the feature male or female. They can use the form of the pronouns as evidence that we understand the referent as being marked by one feature or the other.

For example, in sentence 1 (b) students will see that because *she* can refer to *mother*, but *he* cannot, we must understand *mother* to have the feature [+female], but not the feature [+male]. Since one feature automatically excludes the other, a word like *mother* could also be marked [-male]. This system works very well for the words in group 1, but when students get to group 3, they start to run into trouble. There is no violation of agreement in *The surgeon put on her mask*, so students will want to mark surgeon [+female] (or [-male]). But what about the sentence *The surgeon put on his mask*? If we mark *surgeon* in this sentence [+male] (or [-female]), what are we saying about the word *surgeon*?

Words like *she, he, mother*, and *father* clearly have the feature [+male] or [+female]. Even when we see them out of context, we can predict accurately the form of any pronoun referring to them. But words like *surgeon* and *babysitter* are not clearly either [+male] or [+female] except in very specific contexts. Suggest to students that we might need another way of labeling these words.

One way (the way suggested by Mary Ritchie Key) is to consider [+female] and [+male] *sex* features—features that are clearly related to the biological sex of the people or animals referred to and that are generally mutually exclusive.

For words like *surgeon, babysitter, lawyer, teacher, friend*, we have another grammatical category—*gender*. To mark the gender of a word, we use [+feminine] and [+masculine] (to avoid confusion with the sex features), and these features are far from being mutually exclusive. Since they are rooted in social, not biological, reality, they often occur simultaneously. Unless we have established that the specific lawyer we are talking about is Jane Doe, and not Jonn Doe, *lawyer* is both [+feminine] and [+masculine], and either *she* or *he* will agree with it.

Students should be able to summarize their conclusions in something like the following manner:

She hurt himself violates a grammatical rule and *He is vivacious* violates a semantic rule because *she* can be only [+female] and *he* can be only [+male]. *These words are marked for sex.*

No grammatical rule is violated by:

> The surgeon put on her mask.

or

> The surgeon put on his mask.

and no semantic rule is violated by:

> The surgeon is vivacious.

or

> The surgeon is handsome.

because *surgeon* is both [+feminine] and [+masculine]. *It is marked for gender.*

With this understanding of the difference between sex features and gender features, students can explore the assumptions underlying a variety of words. To start with, they can make one list of all the nouns (and subject pronouns) they can think of that are clearly marked for sex (*he, she, brother, sister, mare, stallion*) and another of all the nouns that are marked for gender (*author, lawyer, dancer, attendant, lighthouse-keeper*), and then discuss the inherent differences between these two groups of words. Special attention should be paid to words, such as *farmer*, which may appear to be just [+male] to some students. Discussion can be open-ended. Students need not draw final conclusions, but they should consider such questions as whether the phrase "the farmer and her husband" violates any grammatical or semantic rules.

You can also ask students to make a list of paired words like *poet/poetess* and *actor/actress*. Have them use the dictionary to find terms that are no longer common, such as *instructress* (*instructor*). Ask students in how many of the cases they use the word without the ending (e.g., *instructor*) to refer to either a man or a woman. Ask what the implications are for pairs like *actor/actress* if words like *instructor* are now assumed to be both [+feminine] and [+masculine].

Again using the dictionary, you can explore the history of pairs like *governor/governess* and *master/mistress*, which are derived from a common base. As the meanings of the two forms diverged in a way that *poet* and *poetess* never did, the *-ess* form developed the feature [+female]. Ask whether *governor* and *master* are also marked for sex. Students should be able to supply a number of similar words used in both masculine and feminine contexts (*She is the master of her fate*).

Finally, ask students what they think the future of words like *policeman* and *salesman* will be, based on what they have learned about gender features. Have them provide examples of sentences in which words like *policeman* and *saleman* refer to both men and women, or discuss whether sentences like *Congressman Sawyer put on her hat* are really ungrammatical, and if so, how we can change them.

A Sex Stereotype Awareness Exercise

Harold D. Sartain
Des Moines Area Community College
Ankeny, Iowa

An activity presented as a study of male-female communication was used with college students to help them develop a better understanding of sex role stereotyping. This particular activity presumes a certain degree of maturity on the part of the students, and it may not be as readily adaptable to younger students as are other practices in this book.

The mere mention of sex stereotyping triggers vocal and subtle physical postures of defense among many of my community college students of English composition and speech fundamentals. They are sophisticated enough in the use of language to think that stereotypes are to be used with some trepidation, if at all, even though they may not have a clear concept of stereotyping. A contemporary male student asked to reveal his stereotype of women might guard against being labelled sexist by replying with an easy and self-deceptive, "I don't stereotype people; I treat everyone as an individual."

To keep a low level of apprehension about communicating openly on the subject of sex stereotypes, I introduce the exercise described below as one concerning male-female communication rather than using the title above. The method is derived from Dr. Herbert A. Otto's "Sex Stereotype Removal" encounter,* which I've adapted liberally for classroom use. The purposes of the exercise are:

1. to enhance awareness of the composition and use of male-female stereotypes in human communication.
2. to facilitate inquiry and communication among men and women on the subject of sex stereotyping.
3. to open the subject of stereotyping to self-examination.
4. to refine concepts of stereotyping.

The exercise begins with the instructor seated with students in a circle, whether in chairs or on the floor. The instructor gives each student a sheet of 8½″ x 11″ paper. He/she announces that the class will participate in an

---

*Herbert A. Otto, *Group Methods to Actualize Human Potential: A Handbook*, 4th limited ed. (Beverly Hills, Calif.: The Holistic Press, 1975), pp. 145-54. The handbook contains many exercises adaptable to classes in communication.

exercise concerning male-female communication. The instructor explains that he/she will have a minor role in the activities and discussions, offering directions and facilitating discussion, but not imposing ideas or evaluating student contributions. (The instructor's role is to give directions and to facilitate open and friendly participation. Hesitancy by students during any part of the process usually signals no more than the need for repeating directions or asking facilitating questions. The instructor should not be critical or coercive.) Then follow the steps below.

1. Instructor: You don't need to write your name on this paper. If you're a female, write in the top margin, "Men are . . . . " Males write in the top margin, "Women are . . . . " Now I'm going to give you five minutes to complete that statement in as many ways as you can think of. Write anything that comes into mind in a list down the paper. For each entry complete the statement *men are/women are* in as few or many words as you need. For example: Men are beer drinkers; women are good drivers; men are dominant in sex; whatever comes to mind. You have five minutes to make your lists as long as you can.

2. Instructor (after three minutes have elapsed): Remember you don't need to think hard or long about these generalizations. Women are fun to be with; men are hard workers; whatever comes to mind. You have a minute or two to continue making your list. (Wait until the end of the five-minute period or stop sooner if all students finish writing.)

3. Instructor: Stop writing and look over your list. What you've written comprises your stereotype, though perhaps not all of it, of the opposite sex. (At this point the instructor may allow him/herself two or three minutes for didactics on stereotyping and for establishing a permissive atmosphere for subsequent steps in the exercise. He/she may wish to offer some defining characteristics of stereotypes. But certainly one objective of the short presentation must be to encourage openness in discussion and to allay possible fears of criticism and censure for participation in the rest of the exercise and discussion of the controversial subject. The instructor must confine him/herself to a maximum of three minutes of talk. For any interested, my "pitch," written pretty much in the informal manner in which I give it, follows.

> Stereotyping is a common mental activity of humans. Stereotypes are collections of generalizations we make about groups of people, and they're modified from time to time as a result of our experiences with people. We most often use them in talking about people as groups rather than as individuals. And, of course, neither all nor part of our stereotype of the opposite sex may apply to each individual of our acquaintance. But stereotypes seem to be here to stay, and we don't always object to them. The problem with them centers around their use in facilitating or blocking human understanding and communication.

Since stereotyping is sometimes a touchy subject, especially in this age of heightened awareness of sexism, some people are reluctant to admit to and think about their own stereotyping behavior. But stereotypes are useful at times. For instance, if our house or apartment caught fire and we called the fire department, we'd probably hope the firefighters would live up to their stereotype of being reliable and "Johnny-on-the-spot," wouldn't we? We wouldn't expect them to arrive forty-five minutes later and then light up and enjoy what was left of the fire. Anyway, if they responded much differently from how we'd expect, we'd probably make some adjustment in our stereotype of firefighters.

Our stereotypes create expectations for other people's behavior. Sometimes they're useful in communication and sometimes harmful. Rather than calling all stereotypes bad, we periodically need to examine the adequacy of our stereotypes and how we use them. Are our stereotypes helping or hindering our relations with others? Are they based on sufficient experience with the stereotyped group? Are they out-of-date? Are they connected with reality? As you know, the exercise we're doing now simply requires us to take a calm, inquiring, and nonjudgmental look at a couple of our stereotypes.

4. Instructor: Now close your eyes (or, if on the floor, lie back and close your eyes). Take a few deep breaths and relax. I'm going to ask you to fantasize for a couple of minutes. I'm going to ask you to have a fantasy of romance. Let your mind drift into a romantic encounter or relationship with another person. You won't be required to share your fantasy with us. Just allow yourself to fantasize for a few minutes. You might want your fantasy to involve another member of this class. Just create the fantasy you want. You have two or three minutes for this. (Allow three minutes for the fantasy and participate too.)

5. Instructor: Let's look again at the *men are/women are* lists. Looking over the lists and thinking about our fantasies, let's answer this question silently to ourselves: Is there a relation between our romantic fantasies and our sex stereotypes? Just think about answering the question for yourself: What relation do you see between your fantasy and your stereotype of the opposite sex? (Allow about a minute.)

6. Instructor: Would anyone like to share his or her fantasy with us? (Probably not.) Did anyone's fantasy involve another member of the class? (Probably a few affirmative responses.)

7. Instructor: There's a general reluctance in our culture to disclose our fantasies and dreams, isn't there? We dream and daydream throughout our lives, yet something tells us not to share or discuss them much publicly. This feeling is aroused especially in connection with our romantic fantasies. We're more inclined to talk about our actual experiences than our fantasies. That may be good or bad or something else, but why is it? I'd just like you to think about whether this inhibition is useful to human beings. In particular, does our reluctance to disclose and discuss our romantic

fantasies promote better understanding and relations among men and women than if the subject were more open to communication?

8. Instructor (select one male and one female): Now the women should pass their papers to   (F)   and the men to   (M)   . I'm going to ask   (M)   to read us the "Men are . . . " lists. Listen for traits that seem to be mentioned several times, though perhaps with different words. (After the lists are read, the instructor appoints another male to go to the blackboard.) There wasn't complete correspondence among the lists, of course, but you observed that many of the generalizations about men cluster around certain traits or characteristics, even though the wordings of the statements were often different. What were some of the recurring ideas in the lists that we can have   (M)   write on the blackboard for reference later? (Students will provide most of them, but the instructor may need to assist by asking questions leading to the identification of other traits.)

9. Thank you   (M)   . Now   (F)   will read us the lists of "Women are . . . . " Listen again for statements that seem to identify similar traits. (Follow the process in Step 8.)

10. You see on the blackboard our group stereotypes of the opposite sex. Notice that in many respects they resemble the more general cultural stereotypes we're familiar with through reading, television, and conversation. What do you think about them? (By this time, most students will be eager to voice opinions. The instructor should channel their energy into the "fishbowl" discussion format in Step 11. Readers unfamiliar with fishbowl discussions need know only that they observe two fundamental rules: participants in the inner circle talk exclusively among themselves while members of the outer circle remain silent observers.)

11. Instructor: We'll handle the discussion in the following manner. All the women form a small circle inside the larger circle. Those of us in the outer circle will remain quiet and listen to your discussion. Just go ahead and share your thoughts among yourselves concerning the men's stereotype of you. What do you think about it? (The women usually need no further direction to encourage lively conversation. However, the instructor should be prepared to restimulate exchange or, more likely, to redirect discussion if it becomes dominated by two or three participants. Useful questions to interject are: Which traits in the stereotype do you think of as being negative or unrealistic? Which elements do you see as positive or realistic? In what ways do you think the male stereotype of women would correspond with your stereotype of your own sex? What traits would you like to see in the stereotype that aren't on the blackboard? Allow a maximum of five minutes for the discussion.)

12. The women return to the outer circle, the men form the inner circle, and the pattern in Step 11 is repeated.

13. Instructor: Reform the large, single circle. Now that each group has heard the other out, we have a few minutes to ask questions of clarification and to share some ideas. In the time remaining, what would you like to say to each other about the opposite sex stereotypes and the fishbowl discussions?

14. Since thinking and discussion about stereotyping will be stimulated by the exercise, and the class period will end before a feeling of completion (in the sense of "settling" the matter) is achieved, the instructor will be in a good position to channel interest in the direction of the next class activity or assignment. However, the exercise is very suitable as a single-period learning activity. The instructor may wish to close with a few brief remarks relative to reexamining and refining the categories of meaning called stereotypes and comment favorably on student participation.

The momentum of the exercise seems to build from caution to squirming to good humor to lively discussion. Step 13 allows for a little debate and venting of energy by students whose competitiveness is held in check earlier. A virtue of the exercise is that it ends on a high energy level rather than beginning and ending in the style of partisanship, acrimony, and unalleviated conflict that students are commonly exposed to in mass media treatments of sex-role stereotyping. One purpose of the exercise is to replace the I don't—she does—they shouldn't syndrome of attack-defense analysis and discussion of stereotyping with a method that fosters self-examination and sharing of ideas in a lively and friendly, yet controlled and productive atmosphere. For whatever reasons, the exercise works to accomplish its purpose.

Methodological Attachment

1. Grade level of students: I've used the exercise successfully with first and second-year community college students. In the fantasy exercise, these students, with whom I had a good rapport, were asked to have a sex fantasy. This approach, originally used by Herbert Otto, has been successful with these college classes, and I would recommend it if the instructor feels it is appropriate.

2. Characteristics of group: The students have been in courses in freshman composition and speech fundamentals. They have been drawn from programs in both career and general education and have ranged in age from 17 to 45 years.

3. When two sections of students were asked to rate anonymously each individual class activity and assignment during the quarter, they gave this exercise an average rating of 3.6 on a scale of 1 to 4 (1, low; 4, high).

4. Drawbacks/possible problems: The only problem I've experienced with the exercise was the reluctance of two male students to do the stereotype

listing. Both protested that they didn't think of people in general terms. I reminded them that they were asked to list general statements about a group, not an individual, and that whatever they chose to write or not to write would be satisfactory. If they did not feel they could do the exercise, they could sit it out. After that, they started writing and became interested participants later in the exercise. They probably wanted some reassurance that their performance would not be evaluated or criticized negatively. It is important for the instructor not to show personal attitudes toward the stereotypes and not to show preferences in response to student contributions. The students must feel free to express their own ideas, not to feel as if they have to please the instructor with them.

It is desirable for students to sit facing each other for more direct communication. However, I should think the exercise could be used with students seated in rows if a provision were made for segregating the discussions in Steps 11 and 12. A formal seating arrangement would influence the outcome of the exercise.

5. How to incorporate: I use the exercise about midway or later in the quarter after students have become acquainted and established an atmosphere of cooperation. I usually use it by itself to create awareness and self-examination in the use of stereotypes. In some classes I follow it up with reading and writing assignments. Currently I follow it with an article on sex-role stereotyping: Linda J. Busby, "Sex-role Research on the Mass Media," *Journal of Communication* (Autumn 1975): 107-131. Included in the article are sex-role stereotypes observed in some commercial television network programs with which I ask my students to compare their own class group stereotypes. Two topics that have been successful stimulators for writing about personal experience in composition classes have been, "An Experience in Being Victimized by Sex Stereotyping," and "A Time When I Misapplied a Sex Stereotype."

I see the exercise as an excellent way of introducing any longer unit on stereotypes of any kind in language and communication; feminism; literature and the mass media; and writing and speaking from personal experience.

Units on Sexism

Individual classroom exercises are a boon to the busy classroom teacher, but often an extended unit, or even a full-length course, is desirable. Five units, developed for high school or college groups, are offered here. Working with these more mature students allows in-depth study of such aspects of sexism as language study, poetry, and images in literature, and strengthens the students' abilities to recognize a pervasive sexist philosophy and understand its dangers.

Three Lessons: Film, Semantics and Composition as Springboards to Studying Sexism

Ruth Lysne
Faribault Senior High School
Faribault, Minnesota

Gerald Kincaid
Minnesota State Department
 of Education

Katherine Joslin
East Leyden High School
Franklin Park, Illinois

In this senior high classroom the film Bonnie
and Clyde, *a song, and the students' parents and
grandparents are resources for instruction
about sex-role stereotyping.*

Many classroom teachers who deal with sex-role stereotyping as revealed in the study of film, language, and literature, advocate integrating this study into the total English curriculum. They feel that isolated units or courses that deal exclusively with the study of sex-role stereotyping tend to result in negative responses. Questioning sex-role definitions along with other ideas that are less threatening tends to reduce the chance for hostile reactions. This should further the ultimate goal of reducing or eliminating society's reliance on stereotypes as a way of defining humans.

The reading materials classroom teachers need for alerting students to sex-role stereotyping are already on the shelves. The viewing materials exist on television, in the video tape library, or in the department's catalog of feature films for a film course. The language materials are created when students do surveys on the connotation or denotation of words in the community. If teachers are aware of the evidence or portrayal of sexism in what they already use, the practice of challenging the validity of sexual stereotyping and modifying its effects on human beings can be developed.

The following lessons, one on the film *Bonnie and Clyde,* another on people's meanings for words, and the third on a personal essay, show how expanding what is already in many a school's curriculum, namely media study or a study of "pop culture," language study, and a writing assignment in a literature course can deal with the question of the validity of sex-role stereotyping. All three lessons were used with senior high students. The lesson on *Bonnie and Clyde* was used in a course entitled *The Short Story and Feature Films* for average or below average readers who needed high interest materials. The course was divided into thematic units, one of which was the study of the causes of violence. The stories in the unit examine how use of stereotyped language such as "the enemy" allows humans to behave in generally unjustifiable ways as is shown in the short story "The Sniper." After the study of this less threatening idea about the destructive potential of stereotypes, the students viewed *Bonnie and Clyde.* The conclusions they drew from discussing the film and how they arrived at them is revealed in the following outline of the lesson. The semantics lesson which had been developed for a language course followed as a means of having the students investigate how forcefully language shapes human perception and how perceptions about expectations based on sex might be broadened.

Lesson One: Bonnie and Clyde

MAJOR ACTIVITY	Analyzing how people respond to film portrayal of men and women through a discovery approach.
GENERAL OBJECTIVE	Critically viewing the portrayal of male and female sex roles in major feature films.
SPECIFIC OBJECTIVE	1. Identifying comparison and contrast of characters in a film as a means of illustrating sex-role limitations.
	2. Recognizing images in film that encourage automatic responses based on sex-role definition.
	3. Distinguishing between a character's action or an event in a film and one's personal response to it on the basis of one's acceptance or lack of acceptance of sex-role stereotyping.
RESOURCES	Television showing of *Bonnie and Clyde.* Film *Bonnie and Clyde.*
CONDITIONS	Room suitable for viewing and small group work.
TIME	Five to six one-hour periods.

PROCEDURE   Stage I
                     View *Bonnie and Clyde* at home or at school
                         (3 hours)
                     Stage II
                     1. Divide into small groups of six students (1 hour)
                     2. Ask each group together to write 20 discussion
                        questions. Each person must contribute at least
                        two questions. No questions are to be rejected.
                     3. Teacher collects questions and overnight com-
                        bines similar questions from all groups.
                     4. Return condensed list of ten questions to each
                        group and each group answers as well as they can
                        (20 min.).
                     5. Groups share answers on all questions but teacher
                        leaves questions on the following topics until last
                        to elicit following points from questions:

STUDENT
QUESTION   Why does the audience react negatively to Blanche
                     and positively to Bonnie?

STUDENT
COMMENTARY   Students recognize their negative response to Blanche
                     immediately and can list why they dislike her.
                     Considering the list, they see she is created as a
                     deliberate contrast to Bonnie, whom they like. She is
                     fearful, unlike Bonnie; she doesn't think under
                     pressure, unlike Bonnie; she conforms to society's
                     moral code, unlike Bonnie; and she is unimagina-
                     tive, unlike Bonnie. Students recognize that Blanche's
                     timidity, her lack of imagination, her lack of cool
                     intelligence, and her conformity to superficial mo-
                     rality make her the traditional female, and yet in the
                     film, Bonnie's untraditional behavior and traits win
                     her audience approval whereas Blanche is rejected.

TEACHER
COMMENTARY   A teacher-directed question as to how the women
                     are alike brings out the basic comparison that
                     determines the women's fates. They both see them-
                     selves primarily in relation to their men. The fate of
                     their husband or lover becomes their fate. Both refuse
                     to leave the side of the men they initially tried to
                     manipulate. Blanche tried to make Buck a law-

abiding citizen and Bonnie saw Clyde as an escape route from a dull, poverty-stricken town. Students discover how the artistic portrayal of sex-role stereotypes alters through comparison and contrast of characters, what would often be their typical response. They are left to ponder to what extent sex-role expectations control human fate.

STUDENT QUESTION

Why were Bonnie and Clyde so destructive as a team when they weren't so dangerous alone?

STUDENT COMMENTARY

Students alone recognize Bonnie's use of her sexuality to attract Clyde as a sex-role stereotype, as well as her stereotyped approval of his violence and power. They also recognize, without help, his substitution of violence for sexual potency, but need teacher direction in formulating a question that deals with violence as the result of fear about masculinity and fear of possible rejection. His insecurity demands increasing use of violence as a means of holding Bonnie. This stereotyped view of how to hold feminine approval is fed by her admiration of stereotyped masculine power. Her companionship and beauty fulfill his need for a visible sign to others of his masculinity. Students can react to the stereotyped view of the male as the powerful aggressor, and the female as the sexual object, who is won through display of power and who then becomes an appendage of the male and shares his fate.

STUDENT QUESTION

Why were Bonnie and Clyde sharing bites of the same piece of fruit before their death?

STUDENT COMMENTARY

As soon as the question is raised, some students see the analogy drawn between Adam, Eve, and the apple, and the loss of innocence. The fruit Bonnie bites and then offers to Clyde moments before their death presents the archetypal image of woman as the object of man's destruction. Prior to this, Clyde's first sexual encounter has stripped him of his "sixth sense" for violence that has saved him before. The use of this image, and the automatic response it brings forth from people brought up in a western sexist culture, can bring about a discussion of images used by filmmakers and writers when they wish to evoke a response based on common cultural myths. Students are left to decide if the film is a deliberate portrayal of the cruel effects of sex-role stereotyping, or if their own increased awareness of sex-role stereotyping has made them sensitive to what the film unconsciously reveals about our society.

Lesson Two

The following lesson on people's responses to words also raises this question about unconscious vs. conscious response. Developed for a unit on semantics, it deals with the power of our meaning for words to shape our perceptions.

MAJOR
ACTIVITY   Analyzing how words affect feelings through the use of survey results.

GENERAL
OBJECTIVE   (Long Range) To determine to what degree people's perceptions are controlled by their meanings for words. ("I can talk about you, but when I do, I'm talking about me.")

SPECIFIC
OBJECTIVE   1. To determine whether "words have meanings for people" or "people have meanings for words."
                        2. To determine how different people react to specific words containing "man"—recording reactions by age and sex.

RESOURCES   Record: "I Wonder"—Ruth Bebermeyer, Community Psychological Consultants (1740 Gulf Drive, St. Louis, MO 63130)

CONDITIONS   Classroom that permits small group work.

TIME   Five 50-55 minute periods, or the equivalent.

PROCEDURE   STAGE I
                        1. Play the song "I Can Talk About You" from the "I Wonder" record listed above (words to song included).

2. Discuss immediate reactions in small groups (4 to 6 per group).
3. Have each group list some of the things we say about others that label people as having desirable or undesirable traits associated with femininity or masculinity, but may be true only in our minds:
   a) She is a tomboy.
   b) She is masculine.
   c) He is effeminate.
   d) He is a sissy.
   e) He/she is selfish, conceited, snobbish, etc.
   f) He/she is kind, fair, just, loving, etc.
   g) He/she likes people, dogs, cats, etc.
   h) He/she is tall, short, fat, etc.
   i) He/she thinks, believes, etc.
4. Compile a master list from subgroups, eliminating duplicates.
5. Classify the kinds of statements recorded:
   a) Inferences stated as fact
   b) Opinions or judgments stated as fact (favorable, unfavorable)
6. Discuss implications of the statements. Identify any that are related to sex (She is a tomboy, He is a sissy, etc.).

STAGE II

1. Using the words, phrases, and statements listed below, have each student write a brief description of the image stimulated by each item.
2. Have each student go back over the list and indicate his/her feeling, positive, negative, or neutral, concerning the image stimulated:

   If no feeling, indicate with a zero.
   If feeling is positive, indicate:
       some—1,   much—2,   very much—3.
   If feeling is negative, indicate:
       some—1,   much—2,   very much—3.

3. Obtain a strength score of feelings for each item by totaling numbers recorded by each student.
4. Compile the results in two groups: those by males, those by females.
5. Analyze and discuss the findings.

STAGE III

1. Using the same list of words, etc., have students survey adults in the community, noting the age and sex of each person surveyed. Try to get an even distribution of age and sex, with a total of approximately 200.
2. Tabulate the results.
3. Analyze and discuss the findings. What are the implications, if any? Is there a need for a change in attitudes, a change in terminology, both or neither?

EVALUATION

What was learned from this project? If needed, how could we change our language behavior? Are any follow-up projects needed?

LIST OF WORDS, PHRASES, AND STATEMENTS FOR REACTIONS AND SURVEY

newsman	author
weatherman	poet
spokesman	singer
policeman	writer
clergyman	sculptor
manpower	fraternize
workmanship	gentleman's agreement
salesmanship	old man
mankind	our forefathers
statesmanship	All men are created equal
layman	honorary fraternity
masterpiece	man hours
brotherhood	old woman
governor	masterful job

Lesson Three: Sex Roles and the American Dream

MAJOR
ACTIVITY

The students are to write an essay identifying their dreams and goals, and how they have been and are being shaped by family sex-role expectations. They are to begin the assignment by interviewing their parents and, if possible, their grandparents.

OBJECTIVES

1. To make students aware of the influence of their parents on their own goals and expectations

through their parents' sex-role expectations.

2. To raise the consciousness of students concerning the relationship of sex roles to individual aspirations.
3. To allow students to see patterns in the lifestyles of people of the same sex and variations according to social class and economic status.
4. To relate such findings to the students' lives.
5. To stimulate communication between students and families.

RESOURCES

The parents and grandparents. Students are to use the following interview questions as the basis for these encounters.

CONDITIONS

It is better to give this assignment early in the study of sexual stereotyping before students have been made aware of its effect. In this way, students will be able to discover for themselves how sexual roles have influenced them personally.

If parents refuse to participate, which sometimes happens, the students should be urged to use other relatives or to fill out the sheet with information they have already heard at home.

TIME

At least two weeks should be given for the assignment, but three would be ideal. The interviews themselves take at least a week, especially if they are discussed in class.

PROCEDURE

Interview

1. What behaviors were expected of you by your parents? What did they want you to do with your life? Did you do this? Why or why not?
2. What were your dreams and goals when you were a teenager? What positive steps did you take to accomplish these goals? How many of them came true?
3. What social, mental, or physical conditions held you back? How would your life have been different if you had been a member of the opposite sex? If you had had more education? If you had had more money?

4. Do you find that your dreams and goals have changed? How? Would you say that who you are and what you have accomplished are satisfying? If not, what other dreams and goals did you have or now still have?
5. Number the following according to how highly you value them. Make number one the thing you value most: money, status, security, education, brotherhood, material possessions, job, religion, family.

Discussion with other students

After the results of interviews have been reported, it enables students to see similarities and differences in patterns. They can see more clearly how sex roles affect the aspirations and achievements of the adults in their community. Have students look for patterns by answering the following questions:

1. What were the dreams and goals of the mothers and grandmothers? Are there similarities? List the jobs women wanted to do, as well as the jobs they finally did.
2. What were the dreams and goals of the fathers and grandfathers? Are there similarities? List the jobs the men wanted to do, as well as the jobs they finally did.
3. Are there differences between the dreams and goals of the women and the men? What did each sex seem to value most? Can you see a difference in values? How can you account for such differences?
4. Do you see yourselves following these patterns? Explain.

Essay assignment

After the interview results are in, students are to complete the following essay assignment dealing with the following items:

1. Compare or contrast your aspirations with those of your parents and grandparents.
2. Trace elements of your aspirations in those of the parent of the opposite sex and the same sex.

3. Compare or contrast conditions which have limited expectations and accomplishments of those in your family and you.
4. How much of you is the result of your own making? What will make you happy and satisfied with your life?

EVALUATION Due to the personal nature of this assignment, it is better not to grade the final paper. The implications seen by the students can be applied to studies of both real and fictional people. Horatio Alger novels are an excellent starting point for a discussion of sex roles and the American dream. They reveal the traditional contrast between the roles of men and women in our society. The female is to remain pure and loyal to her male until he attains a high status. At this point they marry and live happily . . . . As a contrast to this unrealistic how-to-do-it primer, *The Great Gatsby* could also be used. Gatsby follows Alger's myths, which can be discussed in terms of their practicality. Fitzgerald also portrays the contrasting roles of men and women. The treatment of Daisy and Myrtle as well as Daisy's comments about her daughter's prospects as a female in our society should be discussed. Whatever literature is used, the students should be asked repeatedly to draw parallels between the patterns they see in the novels and the patterns they have discovered in their own world.

About Sexist Language: A Unit for High School Students

Carolyn McClintock Peter
Barrington, Rhode Island

As a student teacher, the writer helped thirty senior high school students in a summer enrichment program at Brown University to develop alternatives to sexist language.

"The limits of my language mean the limits of my world." (Ludwig Wittgenstein)

Increased awareness of sexism in language is the goal of this unit on words and the images they convey. It was designed to elucidate ways in which sexism in language narrows our perceptions of one another as well as narrowing our real options in life. I wanted to help my students to become aware that the English language includes many words which either by definition or connotation discriminate against men or women. These words, which exclude or demean one sex or the other, are among the most commonly used words in our language, yet we are not always conscious of the attitudes they communicate. I hoped to suggest in this unit that men and women should be treated primarily as people, linguistically and otherwise, and not primarily as members of one sex or another. My procedure was to avoid insisting upon my own conventions; students would be allowed to discover examples of language which discriminate against either sex and to analyze the implications of this language, perhaps developing alternatives to it.

I began inviting students to talk about their experiences with and attitudes toward sex discrimination. I asked the students if any of them had ever wished to participate in an activity which is usually reserved for the opposite sex. Had they ever been discriminated against because of their sex? Had sex-role stereotypes influenced their behavior? Those few questions stimulated an animated discussion of sexism, a term I then asked the students to define. If someone had not mentioned it, I would have at this point suggested that sexism is limiting to both sexes, not only to women. I defined sexist language as words which discriminate among people on the basis of sex, and I asked the students to work individually to examine the following sentences which I called a "Survey of Awareness of Sexist Language." Some sentences contain sexist language, others reflect sex-stereotyping.

1. The male nurse followed the orders of the woman doctor.
2. The aviatrix had just completed a solo trans-Atlantic crossing.
3. Standard English is spoken by professional people and their wives.
4. I now pronounce you man and wife.
5. Each student will turn in his exam at the end of the hour.
6. Beware: Man-eating sharks swim in these waters.
7. The automobile is one of man's most useful inventions.
8. The chairman introduced the Congressman as a "great American."
9. Using feminine logic, Suzy figured out that she was lost.
10. Pioneers moved West, taking their wives and children with them.
11. Mr. Jones spoke to Miss Evans about the decision.
12. Jim was really the weak sister on the team.

We ended the first day of this unit with a discussion of the different types of sexist language found in these examples. Some students noted that sentences 3, 4, and 10 describe sex-role stereotypes, but do not use sexist language. This distinction, which needs to be made clear if the unit is to be confined to an examination of language, is clarified by the experience of searching for examples of both sexist language and sex-role stereotyping in newspapers and periodicals. This process has the additional effect of demonstrating the pervasiveness of sexist language. I asked my students to find at least one more example of each to share with the class on the second day of the unit.

Some of the most interesting and sensitive comments came out of this exercise. Their search through magazines and newspapers was an enlightening experience because it was so easy to find examples of sexist language. The students' remarks in discussion on the second day of the unit were frequently prefaced by, "I never noticed before . . . " or "I never realized how often . . . . " Many of their examples were variations of the sentences I had presented the day before, but others were shocking in their originality. One student read from a newspaper about a judge who acquitted a man who had been selling sexual services to several regular patrons because, "By definition, a prostitute is a woman." (By the way, in the *Random House Dictionary*, a prostitute is defined as "a person, usually a woman, who engages in sexual intercourse for money.") Another student brought in an advertisement for "Manpower Temporary Services" which pictures a clearly female hand, the index finger of which is decorated as a cute little doll. More forcefully than in our first discussion, the students articulated their various feelings about sexist language. I did not evaluate the students' attitudes, but I encouraged them to develop and to explain their thoughts to each other. The class tended to divide into two groups: those who thought that sexism in language was an important issue, and those who considered it a trivial and unimportant one. Interestingly, both groups contained both sexes.

Following these two days of class discussion, the students worked on independent projects. I had prepared a modified Learning Activity Package which provided the students with provocative ideas, and they were given three class periods in which to work on them and to consult with me. Each student was asked to complete at least three projects by the end of the unit and most students needed to work at home to meet this demand. Not all of the students worked on their projects each day in class, but most activity seemed to be related to sexist language. The two days of class discussion had provoked thought, and a number of debates sprang up spontaneously among small groups of students. This gave them the opportunity to test their ideas against each other. Such informal inter-action helped the students to clarify the issues and caused some of them to alter their thinking about sexist language. A few of the options which I gave them are listed below. Many more could be added or substituted.

1. Make a collection of at least five cartoons which use sexist language and give a brief explanation of why they are sexist.
2. Using fiction books as a source, compile a list of ten adjectives which are usually used to describe men and boys, and another list of those which are usually used to describe women and girls. Suggest the sources of these adjectives.
3. Make a collection of at least five advertisements which use sexist language and give a brief explanation of how it is sexist.
4. Make a list of at least five examples of sexist language which discriminate against men. Rewrite them in a nonsexist form.
5. Give the "Survey of Awareness of Sexist Language" to at least ten people who are not in this class. Combine your results with those of others and report to the class.
6. Look up the following words in dictionaries of English etymology and modern English usage. Make a chart which contrasts the original with the modern meaning. LORD, LADY, MASTER, MISTRESS, PRINCE, QUEEN, MAN, WOMAN.
7. Using the reference books provided, write connotative definitions of the following words: LADY, GENTLEMAN, WOMAN, MAN, SPIN-STER, BACHELOR, FEMALE, MALE, WIFE, HUSBAND, BROAD, STUD.
8. Read either "The Making of a Nonsexist Dictionary" (Alma Graham, *Ms. Magazine* December, 1973), or "The Language of Sexism" (Haig A. Bosmajian, *ETC.: A Review of General Semantics* 29 (1972): 305-313). Write a one-page essay in which you explain why you agree or dis-agree with the statement of the author.
9. Write a statement of at least one page in which you explain and defend your attitude toward current efforts to eliminate sexist words from our language.

I also provided dictionaries, including the *American Heritage School Dictionary* (Boston: Houghton Mifflin, 1972), in which a deliberate effort was made to avoid sexist language, and reference books, such as *The Oxford Dictionary of English Etymology* and Fowler's *Dictionary of Modern English Usage*. A more modern connotative dictionary would have been a helpful addition. The readings mentioned in the list of options were available to the students as was *Language and Woman's Place* by Robin Lakoff (New York: Harper and Row, 1975), an investigation into the roots of words which classify and delineate the sexes. I brought in some children's books which are sexist in language and image (anyone can find these in any children's library), and provided a stack of newspapers and popular magazines, as well as old issues of *Ms.* and *Womansports*. I know of no source books which would be helpful in planning this unit, but the books and articles in the bibliography assisted me.

After three days of less structured class periods, the class came together for a lesson on denotation and connotation in relation to sexist language. We reviewed these terms before I asked the students to consider the denotative and connotative meanings of the following anonymous Victorian jingle:

> Here's a little ditty that you really ought to know:
> Horses "sweat," and men "perspire," but ladies only "glow."

Nearly everyone immediately realized that "sweat," "perspire," and "glow" are similar in denotation, but not in connotation. Some students also noticed that "men" and "ladies" are not parallel terms. I asked them to think of other verbs which are used primarily to describe only men or only women and they came up with "guffaw" and "giggle" or "cackle" for laugh, "talk shop" and "chatter" or "gossip" for talk, and "saunter" and "stroll" for walk. Of course, many adjectives are used exclusively for one sex, but I wanted in this lesson to demonstrate that the connotation of a verb can suggest what is considered to be sex-appropriate behavior. People who "perspire" and "guffaw" are quite different from those who "glow" and "giggle." Connotation defines the stereotype in these examples and in many others the students recalled from experience. They also raised and responded vigorously to questions such as "Why is it that some words, such as 'sprawl' and 'curl up,' seem appropriate only for men or only for women?" "Why does a verb such as 'manage' have one set of connotations when used for a man and another when it is used for a woman?" "What is revealed about a speaker by examining the connotation of his or her language?" Connotation provides a fertile field for students to investigate sexist language. Much could be done with the implied meanings of nouns and adjectives, as well as verbs.

The unit ended with a short quiz in which the students were required to identify examples of sexist language, to describe in what way they are sexist, and to rewrite the sentences containing them in a nonsexist form.

The sentences were similar to the ones used in the first exercise, but the students were expected to be more sophisticated in their treatment of them. Everyone knew where the sexist language was located and how to change the sentences to avoid it. Not everyone could describe how the language discriminated against men or women.

I also asked students to evaluate the unit and to analyze its effect upon them. A great majority wrote that the unit was interesting, and almost all of them said that they had become more aware of sexist language. One student wrote, "Thank you for opening our eyes." Some indicated that the greater awareness had led to a new attitude about sexist language. To me, the comments which best demonstrated the success of the unit were those which indicated that the students had come to understand each other better. One young man commented, "I never realized how strongly women would feel over some words." A young woman wrote, "It was interesting to watch the boys' reaction to this unit." Another student said, "I like the discussions and the way I found out how other people feel." The students' greater comprehension of each other, their increased knowledge of semantics, and enhanced social consciousness, indicate the value of a unit on sexist language for high school students.

References

Crowley, Sharon. "The Semantics of Sexism." *ETC.: A Review of General Semantics* 30 (1973): 407-411.

McGraw-Hill Book Company. *Guidelines for Equal Treatment of the Sexes in McGraw-Hill Book Company Publications*. New York. Available from the publisher (1221 Avenue of the Americas, New York, N.Y. 10020).

Nilson, Alleen Pace. "Sexism in English: A Feminist View." In *Female Studies VI: Closer to the Ground*, by Nancy Hoffman et al. Old Westbury, N.Y.: The Feminist Press, 1972.

Stacey, Judith et al. *And Jill Came Tumbling After: Sexism in American Education*. New York: Dell Publishing Company, 1974.

Strainchamps, Ethel. "Our Sexist Language." In *Woman in Sexist Society*, edited by Vivian Gornick and Barbara K. Moran. New York: Basic Books, Inc., 1971.

Sutton, William A. *Sexual Fairness in Language*. 1973. Available from the author (English Department, Ball State University, Muncie, Indiana 47306, 35¢ per copy).

Language and Sex Stereotyping

Mildred Jeffrey
Hofstra University
Hempstead, Long Island, New York

This course on sexism in language contains exercises adaptable to language and literature courses on various levels, emphasizing the relationship of language to behavior.

My Hofstra University undergraduate course on sexism in language could be easily adapted for junior or senior high school students. Even I am continually modifying it on the basis of student evaluations required at the end of each semester. The important thing is to work toward student recognition of sex-role stereotyping for both males and females. The basic framework of the course consists of a series of lectures on aspects of language, preparing students to conduct an extended survey of a particular area of language use. Findings were summarized orally in class and then written out at some length to be handed in as a substitute for a final exam.

The first time around I asked the students to keep a journal and report weekly on the following:

1. examples of sexist behavior by self or contemporaries
2. examples of sexist language by self or contemporaries
3. examples of spoken sexist language by persons other than contemporaries (e.g., professor, parent, store owner, newscaster, doctor, etc.)
4. examples of sexist language in print (magazine advertising, newspapers, textbooks, literature, etc.)

Each example was annotated as to context and sex of speaker or writer. Many instances of unexpected stereotyping by the students came to light during the lively discussions set off by the reading of the journal entries.

The second time the course was offered, I asked the students to bring in, read, and comment upon relevant newspaper items each week. The third time, I tightened the structure by relating the weekly assignments more closely to the lecture topics. This proved to be the most satisfactory in that it eliminated the kind of repetition which comes with random sampling by the students.

At all times we reminded ourselves that "sexist" language (which includes phrases and sentences as well as single words) and the stereotyping that language both reflects and causes come in several varieties: that which denigrates (dumb blonde) or flatters (my better half), that which points out the sex where it should be irrelevant (lady judge), and that

which assumes one sex or the other where such assumption is uncalled for
(the nurse . . . she; the mechanic . . . he). Obviously, some differentiating
words are not sexist (father, mother) if they are purely descriptive and do
not rob us of any options.

Here are some of the weekly assignments and the areas of investigation
for the term projects.

1. Generally speaking, which of the following character and personality traits are associated with men and which with women? (In deciding
upon your answer, be sure to think about people at large—as reflected in
the media, for example—rather than about your own friends and
acquaintances. In other words, what are the stereotypes?) Underline in red
the traits associated with males and in green those associated with females.
Which collection, the red or the green, reflects the "strong" or "healthy"
personality that is supposed to be better equipped for the vicissitudes of
life? Think about the relationship between these traits and the way little
boys and little girls are treated.

Behavior more aggressive	Behavior less aggressive
Opinionated	Rather easily persuaded
Self-reliant	Dependent
Talkative	Rather silent
Noisy	Quiet
Stubborn	Flexible
Outgoing	Shy
Logical	Emotional
Realistic	Unrealistic
Ambitious (get ahead)	Not particularly ambitious
(What I will be?)	(Whom will I marry?)
Money-oriented	People-oriented
Career-oriented	Life-centered
Blunt	Tactful
Religious	Not particularly religious
Serious	Frivolous
Capable	Rather helpless
Practical	Artistic
Helps others voluntarily	Does not volunteer help
Has physical endurance	Wilts quickly
Persistent	Easily discouraged
Dignified	Playful
Assertive	Questioning
Matter-of-fact	Imaginative
Concerned with fundamentals	Superficial
Rough	Gentle
Concerned with personal	Not particularly concerned with
appearance	personal appearance
Tuned in to the reactions of	Not particularly tuned in to the
others	reactions of others
Steadfast	Changeable

2. Observe people in face-to-face verbal communication. Then next to each of the terms below, write M if the activity seems to be more characteristic of males, F if more characteristic of females, and M/F if characteristic of both sexes. In addition, write C if it is an activity indulged in chiefly by children. Do you come up with any interesting combinations?

bragging	whining
teasing	blurting
flirting	ranting
explaining	chatting
ordering	gossiping
requesting	sneering
browbeating	criticizing
inquiring	praising
nagging	blaming
patronizing	whispering (secrets)
pontificating	telling jokes
narrating	making puns
scolding	lecturing
needling	making small talk
hinting	complaining
insinuating	interrupting
lying	challenging
fibbing	agreeing
arguing	flattering
denying	defying
sermonizing	nitpicking

3. Archetypes and Symbols. Next to each item write the adjective or noun which suggests the trait(s) underlying the role. (For example, Amazons—warlike women). Summarize your conclusions about each column.

Women	*Men*
Antigone	The Hero
The Crone	The Anti-Hero
The Enchantress	Messiah
Earth Mother	God the Father
Mother Nature	The Son of God
The Fates	The Holy Child
The Muses	Zeus, Jupiter
Eumenides	The Prodigal Son
Bacchae	Faust
The Scarlet Woman	The Devil, Satan, Mephistopheles
The Whore of Babylon	The Villain (in old melodramas)
The Bitch Goddess Success	The Trickster, Wily One
The Temptress	Father Time
Eve	Father Sky
Lilith	Dionysius
Helen of Troy	Bacchus

Demeter	Oedipus
Persephone	Orpheus
Cordelia	The Victorian Father
Medea	The Heavy (in a play)
Portia	The Dictator
Circe	The Tyrant
The Lorelei	General, Generalissimo
Jezebel	Con Man, Flim Flam Man
The Blessed Mother Mary	The Pimp
The Blessed Virgin	Bandit, Highwayman
Phaedra	Lone Ranger
Griselda	The Sheriff
The Wife of Bath	Knight in Shining Armor
Gypsy Bawd	Knight on a White Horse
Shiksa	Lord of the Manor
Squaw	Boss, Chief
Tomboy	Man about Town
Siren	Big Man on Campus
Vamp	Stud
Moll	Playboy
Bachelor Girl	Galahad
Spinster	Christ
Old Maid	The Executive, Man in Gray
Golddigger	Flannel Suit
J.A.P. (Jewish-American Princess)	Machiavelli
Jewish Mother	Don Quixote
Delilah	Casenova
Xanthippe	Don Juan
The Great White Goddess (see	Football Hero
Robert Graves)	The Rake
Electra	Prometheus
Primadonna	Mars
Little Orphan Annie	Wodin
Dumb Dora	Dagwood
Blondie	Walter Mitty
Fallen Woman	Clown
Poor Butterfly	Life of the Party

4. In each of the following sections, explain the connection between the quotation and the language sample. Add another sample to each.

  a) "We see and hear and otherwise experience very largely as we do because the language habits of our community predispose certain choices of interpretation."[1]

  (1) "Dr. Benson is covering for Dr. Smith today."
      "Well, is he just as good?"

---

1. Edward Sapir as quoted by Benjamin Whorf, "The Relation of Habitual Thought and Behaviour [sic] to Language," in *Language in Thinking*, ed. Parveen Adams (Baltimore: Penguin Books, 1972), p. 123.

b) "... a language ... is an inventory of the concerns and interests of those who employ it at any given time .... "[2]
  (1) "Liberty, equality, fraternity" was the motto of the French Revolution.
  (2) The program will be presented as part of the observance of National Brotherhood Week.

c) "Language behavior feeds back upon the social reality that it reflects and helps to reinforce it (or to change it) in accord with the values and goals of particular interlocutors."[3]
  (1) Boys don't cry.
  (2) Boys are so rough.

d) "The meaning of every word [or phrase] is a generalization or a concept .... "[4]
  (1) "I now pronounce you man and wife."
  (2) He moved his family to St. Louis.

5. Forms of Words and What Form Tells Us. Free associate to the following pairs of words by jotting down next to each the first three or four things that come to mind *before you stop to think and begin to discard or modify.* Analyze the results. Can you make any connection between the form of the words and the comments you put down?

master	nurse
mistress	male nurse
governor	author
governess	authoress
doctor	poet
woman doctor	poetess
lawyer	usher
lady lawyer	usherette
waiter	girl
waitress	gal
busman	
busboy	

Do you find the following sentences acceptable or unacceptable? Why or why not?

a) Barbara Tuchman, authoress of *The Guns of August,* is a widely recognized historical writer.
b) Emily Dickinson, the New England poetess, occupies a secure place in the pantheon of American writers.

2. Joshua A. Fishman, *The Sociology of Language* (Rowley, Mass.: Newbury House Publ., 1972), p. 166.
3. Fishman, p. 170.
4. L.S. Vygotsky, "Thought and Word," in *Language in Thinking,* p. 181.

6. Explain the stereotyping behind each of the following:

    a) the old ball and chain
    b) a sweet young thing
    c) Hi, Doll.
    d) husband-hunting
    e) husband-dumping (from a newspaper headline about women seeking divorces)
    f) What a dish!
    g) a gorgeous hunk of man
    h) trying to catch a man
    i) "The farmer takes a wife"

7. What is the stereotyping in each of the following news items from *The New York Times*? Is the stereotyping explicit or implicit?

a) from a news story by a woman reporter about the British Conservative Party leader:

> "The most operative word is lady—old-fashioned, proper, traditional lady," said a woman who heard her speak at a private luncheon . . . . "She is a flower among thorns . . . . "
>
> "She was prettier than I expected, softer, younger," said Barbara Walters, who interviewed her . . . .
>
> Mrs. Thatcher, who cooks breakfast every morning for her husband, is irritated by questions on feminism but is well aware that she could be the first woman Prime Minister in English history.

b) from a column by P.L. Travers, author of *Mary Poppins*:

> The prototypes [women's role models in Grimm's *Fairy Tales*] are endless and there is no woman alive who cannot be assimilated to one or another of them. When one is confronted with such manifold powers and possibilities, attempting to assassinate a President, becoming a Madison Avenue executive, or holding up a bank teller with a machine gun seem poor cheap kinds of activity—fit only for men.

c) from a news item about a rich family in Lisbon after the revolution:

> "It's shocking that these strong young boys have nothing to do" [a mother speaking angrily about her sons who are now out of work]. "The four daughters," she said, "have no history," meaning that like most upper-class Portuguese women they are married and have children and that's that.

8. Underline the stereotyping language in the following nursery rhymes and then summarize the differences between the male and female roles. (Selections used were these: "Sing a song of sixpence," "What are little boys made of," "Little Miss Muffet," "Georgie Porgie," "Polly put the kettle on," "Little Polly Flinders," "Peter, Peter, pumpkin eater," "Mary, Mary, quite contrary," "Rock-a-bye-baby," "When I was a little

boy," "Mother, may I go out to swim," "Charley Barley, butter and eggs," "Little Dickey Dilver," "Ladybird, ladybird, fly away home," "When Jacky's a good boy.")

9. Are the sex roles indicated in the following selections usual or unusual? Look through a dictionary of quotations and find ten more examples of stereotyping.

> a) Frailty, thy name is woman.—Shakespeare
> b) Who can find a virtuous woman? For her price is far above rubies.—Proverbs 31:10
> c) The souls of women are so small,
>   That some believe they've none at all.—Samuel Butler
> d) For the husband is the head of the wife, even as Christ is the head of the church: and he is the saviour of the body. Therefore as the church is subject unto Christ, so let the wives be to their own husbands in every thing.—Ephesians 5:23-24
> e) Man's love is of man's life a thing apart;
>   'Tis woman's whole existence.—Byron
> f) Worth makes the man.—Pope
> g) I dare do all that may become a man—Shakespeare
> h) La Belle Dame sans Merci
>   Hath thee in thrall.—Keats

Suggestions for Areas of Investigation for Language and Sex Stereotyping

Contemporary song lyrics
Traditional song lyrics
Greeting cards
Current movie(s)
Old movie(s)
Rock musical(s)
Traditional Broadway musical(s)
Off-Broadway play(s)
Broadway play(s)
Newspaper editorial content (news, features, columns, editorials, sports)
Newspaper ads (display or classified)
Cartoons
Comic Strips
The language of engagements and weddings (announcements, ads)
Conversations by particular groups or in particular situations
Children's stories
Novels (by a particular author)
Poetry (a particular poet or particular genre, e.g., the Elizabethan love lyric)
The Bible

Self-help books, manuals on how to improve your life
Oratory—religious or political
Textbooks (by grade level, by subject)
Radio program(s) (commentary, news, drama, comedy, etc.)
TV program(s)
Radio advertising (kind of product)
TV advertising (kind of product)
Magazine ads—limit investigation to one kind of magazine or one kind of
    product
Publicity releases or promotional material distributed by banks, depart-
    ment stores, etc.

Women's Lives—Mirrors and Models

Lynn Z. Bloom
University of New Mexico
Albuquerque, New Mexico

*College students study biographies and
autobiographies that introduce them to
outstanding women with diverse images and roles.*

Creative. Intelligent. Self-reliant. Dynamic. Self-confident. With occasional exceptions, strongly positive and able to cope with the vicissitudes
of fate and fortune. So the women studied in my course, "Images of Women
in Biography and Autobiography," knew themselves, sometimes from very
young ages. So the world knows them now. So are students delighted to
discover them, for not only are these women fascinating in their own right,
but they break the old images and smash the stereotypes of passive,
dependent, subservient, unproductive, neurotic women so often proffered
in twentieth-century fiction by and about women. Emphasizing through
biography and autobiography the positive images of effective women who
have actually lived, and with whose lives the students can identify, is
intrinsically stimulating, and a valuable source of role models for readers
of either sex, and of any age or level in college.

Purposes

"Images of Women in Biography and Autobiography" is intended to:
1. Introduce the students to a variety of actual outstanding, memorable women of diverse images and roles.
2. Present distinguished examples of literature in the genres of biography and autobiography.
3. Familiarize the students with issues, problems, techniques, and materials of the genres of biography and autobiography, through reading and through projects involving their own or others' life history, as either an individual or a member of a family, social, cultural, intellectual or occupational group.

This course also helps the students to learn about themselves; the women students especially value this biographical perspective on their actual and potential roles and images as women. In others they see themselves.

Format and Content

The semester-long course proceeds as follows. All the books are available in paperback.

Week I: Biography and Autobiography as Genres

Considerations of biography and autobiography as genres include various techniques of writing biography: characterization of the subject and those in her sphere; methods of assessing biographical accuracy; proportioning and emphases on selected aspects, incidents, characteristics of one's life or personality; uses of themes, symbols, dialogue, quotations from others who knew or wrote about the subject. We also examine matters of special relevance to biographies of *women*, such as whether any emphasis has been given to female biology, psychology, familial or cultural roles; to the subject's physical appearance (including beauty or its absence); to her love life and/or relationships with her parents and her children. If the woman has combined a career with a family, what is the perceived relationship between the two?

As a practical—and most illuminating—exercise, the students analyze a mimeographed collection of the raw materials of biography: letters written to, by, and about the same person; bills, telegrams, receipts, photographs, and other relevant documents. The class decides how to interpret these: what proportion to give to the times, the milieus, and the motivations of the various letter writers; how to accommodate not only what is said but what is in between the lines—and how to deal with deviations from standard grammar and spelling. In the process, they are amazed to realize the multitude of options—ways to handle or to interpret even the most innocuous or apparently unarguable "fact." And so the students begin to learn the biographer's art.

In the subsequent weeks which focus on the literary works, it is very effective to discuss the books in pairs; each student reads one of a pair which treat similar roles, images, careers, or stages in life. Class discussion then focuses not only on the individual works and lives, but on comparisons and contrasts between them. (However, in a more elementary course a single book in common would be preferable.)

Week II: Woman Developing

Do women in the western world (or universally) have a common pattern of development? What determines how a woman matures and who or what she will become as an adult? How significant is the presence or absence of a happy childhood, or familial or economic security? What are the effects of freedom and restraint on a developing girl? Of what does a "good" education consist—and for what does it educate?

Two autobiographies permit a particularly meaningful exploration of these questions: Mary McCarthy's *Memories of a Catholic Girlhood* (1957) and Maya Angelou's *I Know Why the Caged Bird Sings* (1970). Both emphasize women in their roles as preschool children; as granddaughters with absent or deceased mothers; as schoolgirls with significant relations with their peers and siblings; as young women maturing psychologically, socially, and sexually.

Week III: Mothers and Daughters

What does it mean to be a daughter? a mother? Are there any elements common to these roles at a given time? Are there any intergenerational changes? Must there be conflict or abrasiveness between mothers and maturing daughters? What are the options for relationships between adult daughters and their aging mothers? Simone de Beauvoir's intellectually analytic *Memoirs of a Dutiful Daughter* (1959) examines a number of these issues. It is a foil to Jane Howard's touching *A Different Woman* (1973). Howard anatomizes and juxtaposes the relationships between her sister, her mother, and herself, with biographical vignettes of other women emerging into feminist consciousness. Lives touch, and flow, and change, and touch again.

Week IV: Woman as Sex Object/Wife

To what extent do women choose either role or the dimensions of each? To what extent are such roles imposed upon them—by men, other women, their society? If a woman is a sex object or a wife, can she be anything else?

What problems or satisfactions does the performing of either of these roles provide? Are these roles incompatible?

One of the books in this category, Nancy Milford's *Zelda* (1970) focuses on the high-strung and ultimately paranoid-schizophrenic wife of F. Scott Fitzgerald. She is the negative exception to the many positive images of woman depicted in most of the other biographies studied in this course. Zelda's frenetic functioning as a teenage sex object, followed by her frustrated subordination to her famous husband's larger ego and talent, contributed to her psychic frailty. Antithetical to Zelda are Mrs. Horace Mann and Mrs. Nathaniel Hawthorne, two of the three *Peabody Sisters of Salem* (1950), energetic and effective heroines of Louise Hall Tharp's meticulous group portrait, not only of the three sisters and their two famous husbands, but of the entire mid-nineteenth century New England intellectual milieu.

If the class wishes to compare group biographies, Nigel Nicolson's sympathetic *Portrait of a Marriage* (1973) details three strong and haunting personalities of Vita Sackville-West, her husband, Harold Nicolson, and her sometime lover, Violet Trefusis.

Week V: Woman as Entertainer

Also related to women as sex objects are women entertainers, especially if they are film stars, actresses, or pop singers. The images of many of these women were deliberately molded by their directors, managers, or publicity agents—almost always men. So the reader of these biographies and autobiographies may appropriately question the extent to which a contrived public image reflects the woman's actual personality. To what extent does the woman mold her life to fit the image of the tramp, the vamp, the femme fatale, the "it" girl, the Sunshine Girl, the girl-next-door, the Mata Hari, the Happy Hooker? Does the onstage myth become the offstage reality, or does a public Dr. Jekyll conceal a private Ms. Hyde? Similar questions might be asked of politicians' wives, who function primarily as adjuncts of their husbands.

Accurate answers to these questions are difficult to obtain unless one reads multiple biographies of the same person, such as the several volumes on Lady Bird Johnson. Even then the group may be unreliable; consider the various unauthorized lives of Jacqueline Kennedy Onassis. At times the unreliability is intensified when the same people who create the images write the biographies, or collaborate with the subject on "autobiographies." Sometimes coauthors are acknowledged; Charles Samuels helped Ethel Waters with *His Eye Is On the Sparrow* (1950). But did Gypsy Rose Lee, Hedy Lamarr, Mary Astor, and Lillian Roth (among others) write every word of their own *Lives*? They are as discreet about their authorship as about their ages! As a group, such authors are not distinguished as writers, raconteurs, or scholars, and their books are of lesser quality than the authoritative volumes in the rest of the course.

Week VI: Woman as Representative of a Race, Culture, or Ethnic Group

To what extent can a woman's life be seen as larger than any individual life? To what extent is a woman representative not only of herself but of her race, culture, ethnic group, or nationality? Perhaps the answers lie in the extent to which the woman has to cope or contend with her race or background as they affect her life—or with her life as it impinges on these. The autobiographies of black Civil Rights activist Anne Moody, *Coming of Age in Mississippi* (1962) and Brazilian slumdweller Carolina Maria de Jesus (also black), *Child of the Dark* (1962) are penetrating and moving commentaries on social and cultural forces, as well as on individuals. They reveal women who have had to struggle for the fundamental human rights to dignity and a peaceful, benign life that are often denied to members of their racial or lower economic group, whatever their nationality. These women are resourceful, pragmatic idealists, and super strong; they've had to be—not just to survive, but to prevail.

Week VII: Woman as Personality/Intellect

Can the force of a woman's deviant intellect or personality mold society to accommodate her individuality? To what extent is she obliged to meet its norms? What are the consequences of social or artistic deviation—ostracism, exile, an untimely death—or fame? Does it take a strong personality to be an artistic innovator? Strong and deviant in personality or intellect (or both) are Myra Friedman's Janis Joplin in *Buried Alive* (1973) and Gertrude Stein's self-portrait in the unique *Autobiography of Alice B. Toklas* (1933). Joplin's fire and pathos are superbly re-created by her former PR agent, a notable exception to authors of that type. In contrast is the humor and egotism of Stein, who cleverly masks her own insouciance through the ventriloquizing persona of her doppelganger, Alice B. Toklas.

Week VIII: Women as Authors

Talent aside, are the lives of women authors different in any significant ways from the lives of women—or men—who are not authors? Are the lives of women in professions that require dedication, creativity, and self-imposed discipline different from the lives of women whose activities do not? What makes a writer? To what extent are contacts with other authors or involvement in a literary milieu helpful or necessary? Will talent always emerge and be recognized? Since writing is essentially a quiet, private, undramatic activity, how can one write an interesting biography or autobiography of a literary figure?

Lillian Hellman's *An Unfinished Woman* (1969), though itself unfinished, and Colette's *Earthly Paradise* (1966), unusual, as its subtitle indicates, because it is an *Autobiography Drawn from the Writings of Her Lifetime*, provide partial answers to these questions. Both volumes, particularly Colette's, show women emerging as evocative and powerful writers in control of their own adult lives and careers after early existences of pain, tumult, and uncertainty dominated by others.

Week IX: Women as Rulers

Can the hand that rules the world also rock the cradle? Is a woman ruler expected to exploit (or safeguard) her sexuality for political purposes? Is her reign subject to any special consideration or limitations because of her femininity? How does a woman with access to influence and power and money relate to men of comparable status? Can she, need she, ever be one of the "boys" in the smoke-filled back room?

Considering the controversiality of various notable women rulers, this topic lends itself particularly well to a comparison of two or more biographies of the same woman. Such a comparison provides multiple interpretations of personality and motives, multiple reflections and refractions of an image, multiple insights into the "selected fictions" which compose the lives of any person. Multiple biographies of famed women rulers are abundant; the readers usually know something about the rulers' lives to test against the biography. Lytton Strachey's somewhat Freudian, debunking *Elizabeth and Essex: A Tragic History* (1928) is an intriguing foil to Elizabeth Jenkins's more thoroughgoing and balanced *Elizabeth the Great* (1958). Students intrigued by the redoubtable Victoria might compare Elizabeth Longwood's scholarly *Queen Victoria: Born to Succeed* (1964) with the equally scholarly but fast-paced *Queen Victoria* (1972) by Cecil Woodham-Smith.

Week X: Woman as Social Activist

It would be mere rhetoric to ask, in this Year of the Woman, whether women have in fact been effective as social activists. Yet the *images* of women activists, such as Amelia Bloomer, Carry Nation, and Margaret Sanger, are particularly interesting because they are so often in opposition to the safe status quo which is conventionally thought to be "woman's place," if not woman's fate. Are such women more "masculine" than their less energetic, less socially conscious sisters? Are they necessarily bizarre, ludicrous, or threatening? Can—and do—they work effectively with men, or are their efforts primarily in a separate woman's arena, of their own choosing or not? How are they regarded by the general public, whose lives their efforts are meant to effect? How are they treated by the law, and by law-enforcers (usually men), with which they are often in conflict?

Biographies and autobiographies of women social activists provide varied answers to these questions, as well as penetration into the social and political aspects of the cultures that impinge on these women. Such women are often positive models for burgeoning feminists, which many students become in the process of learning about the lives of notable women.

Richard Drinnon's comprehensive life of anarchist Emma Goldman, *Rebel in Paradise* (1961), enables readers to recognize that the many impediments to political and sexual equality and to social justice that existed in the early twentieth century are still with us today. It also reveals that many efforts for social reform, no matter how well-intentioned or dedicated or forceful the adherents, do not necessarily succeed. Comparable defeats, though with more successes, are described in Joseph Lash's fascinating biographies of Eleanor Roosevelt: *Eleanor and Franklin* (1971) and *Eleanor: The Years Alone* (1972). Eleanor was a dynamic and extremely well-informed woman, but despite her many accomplishments and her access to power, she did not always have sufficient authority or influence in her own right to make the social changes she desired.

Week XI: The Liberated Woman

It is particularly illuminating to understand the life of a liberated woman and how she grew. Was she liberated from birth? If so, how? If not, through what process did she become an autonomous, fully-functioning woman? Do all liberated women have some attitudes or behaviors in common? Can such women become role models for their aspiring readers?

Maragaret Mead's *Blackberry Winter: My Earlier Years* (1972) provides one strong woman's answers to these questions. She applies her anthropologists's perspective to the tribal, parental, and cultural influences on her formative years and demonstrates how both her adult life style and the practice of her vocation reflect the independence of mind, self-assertive will, and strength of character instilled in her at an early age. Shirley MacLaine's *Don't Fall Off the Mountain* (1970) presents the liberation, and the professional successes, without Mead's useful analyses or exploration of problems.

Week XII: Issues and Images: An Overview—Virginia Woolf's Orlando

Is it possible to capture the "truth" of a life? Is the "real person" contained in the essence of the "six or seven selves" that the biographer selects from the subject's many thousand? How can a biographer know, let alone re-create and interpret, the subject's state of mind or motivations at any given time? What meaningful connections can the biographer make between the subject's mental and physical activities?

Orlando (1928), Virginia Woolf's treatise on (among other matters) biographical theory and sex roles and their relation to time and culture, explores these issues in amusing and fascinating detail. Consequently, although it is a work of fiction, *Orlando* fittingly highlights the philosophical and technical issues of life-writing, and serves as an appropriate finale for the course. Moreover, Orlando's change of sex from a man to a woman midway through the narrative dramatically emphasizes the course's focus on images, and permits an exploration of these from the perspectives of both sexes, as well as from the point of view of a depersonalized, asexual narrator. (Though for a touching analysis of a real person's change of images and roles through change of sex, see Jan Morris's autobiographical *Conundrum* [1974].)

Course Management

The remainder of the semester is devoted to student reviews of biographies (early); discussions of techniques of life-writing, historical research, and oral interviewing (throughout the semester, interspersed with the readings); and presentations of student term projects (late). By then, the students have examined a multiplicity of images of women. They have seen how various published authors have coped with the diverse issues and materials of life-writing, and can apply this knowledge to their own work.

Students who do not wish to discuss or reveal their own lives in these projects are in no way obliged to do so. They can always confine their research to relatives, friends, or safe (perhaps safely dead) others. Nevertheless, many students do write autobiographies, particularly older women who want to gain perspective on the difficulties in their own lives. These occasionally lead to chauvinistic husbands' angry objections to their wives' unflattering portraits or marital analyses. The only other problems I've observed in the course are the difficulties that younger students have in writing about their age peers whose lives closely resemble their own; familiarity breeds myopia and obtuse or self-serving interpretations.

No special materials or resources except the texts themselves are required. However, if the raw materials that comprise a life are available for scrutiny, so much the better: diaries (see Moffatt and Painter, *Revelations: Diaries of Women*, 1974); letters, family photographs, newspaper clippings, scrapbooks, films (Joyce Chopra's *Joyce at Thirty Four* is an entertaining, deceptively simple filmed autobiography), as well as personal recollections tape-recorded or told "live." Every woman, every person, is an evanescent specimen, if not a vanishing species, to be protected and preserved while the raw materials are still available.

Conclusion

Such strong, effective, interesting subjects of the biographies and autobiographies discussed here are exhilarating to meet, and inspiring to get to know—especially presented as they are, through books whose literary qualities match the zest, grace, wit, and perspicacity of the subjects. The students, women especially, never fail to make parallels—or to note (with sorrow or joy) the discrepancies—between the lives of these women and their own. For the most part, they see these women as heroines in the drama of ordinary—and extraordinary—life, to be applauded or respected and sometimes to be pitied. The students are so stimulated that they write papers of extraordinary quality (some have since been published) and consistently engage in the liveliest and most engrossing class discussions I've been privileged to lead.

These biographical and autobiographical works—and courses—are literally a matter of life, not death. The works that I've discussed here not only explain and interpret roles and images of positive lives, but they inspire and redefine positive images of women for the lives of innumerable students seeking self-identity and self-fulfillment—which their notable predecessors have already found.

American Women Poets: A Course Unit

Jeanne H. Kammer
Wheeling College
Wheeling, West Virginia

A poetry unit for college students provides a study of the work of fourteen American women whose poems offer "technical mastery as well as socio-psychological records of female experience."

Current literature courses devoted exclusively or partially to women writers and their concerns suffer from several drawbacks the tendency to organize the literature thematically around what are perhaps stereotypical categories determined by content; the avoidance of the issue of a character-istic manner or form in women's writing, often the avoidance of form altogether; and, perhaps most acute, the problem of selecting a work that is technically first-rate as well as thematically or socially significant.

This course unit, growing out of the thesis that major women poets of the last century have exhibited a similarity of manner as well as common characterisitics of theme, images, and *persona*, represents an effort to reorganize the standard thematic emphasis, confront the issue of form, and offer to the college student a selection of poems by women which are examples of technical mastery as well as a socio-psychological record of female experience. The unit provides, I believe, a more genuinely literary handling of these writers than is usually the case, and a more provocative one in the questions it raises concerning the relationship between the artist, her somatic and psychological nature, her cultural setting, and the nature of her art.

The five subdivisions represent a progressive exposition of these questions: First, the common experience of the woman artist as a "misfit," a "maverick" according to her perception of the roles assigned to females in the culture and according to society's views of her personally; second, her reaction to this experience and what it involves of isolation, pain, oppression, betrayal—the instinct for compression, camouflage, sub-mersion in form as a means of protection, strength, and, ultimately, freedom; third, the growing perception of and desire to escape the stigmatizing name of "poetess" and the consequent effort to avoid excessive emotion or overstatement of any sort; fourth, the cumulative record, beneath the compressed and oblique manner, of an emerging female consciousness, exhibited in the growing confidence of female themes and voices; and finally, the sense of heritage and commonness among the women poets of these decades, particularly in the last twenty years.

In each section I have provided an initial prose selection designed to focus on specific issues and provoke discussion of the poems which follow; I have also gathered together poems which I believe will survive close reading as well as serve to illustrate the ideas under discussion. Six major poets (Dickinson, H.D., Moore, Bishop, Plath and Levertov) are heavily represented throughout the unit, since they provide together the recog-nizable outline of a compressive tradition in women's work. Others among their contemporaries are included as they echo and enlarge this general tendency. For each section, I have chosen works accessible to the average college or community college student, but still well worth the time of the English major.

The task of the instructor within and beyond this unit will be to provide the larger historical and literary context within which the evolution of women's poetry has taken place, according to his or her own vision of the American tradition and the nature of other units in the larger course structure. The chronological arrangement of poems within each section is meant to encourage the exploration and discovery of links and influences, as well as the relationship of the individual poet to the prevailing literary fashion of her generation.

In the end, the student should come away with an understanding of the singularity and special problems of the woman poet; a familiarity with a number of very good poems by women; a reasonably accurate knowledge of their historical and literary context and the influences which shaped their work; and the ability to read compressive poems with a sensitivity to their habits of "not-saying" that should improve the ability to read poems in general. With these objectives, the unit could easily be adapted to suit courses in poetry, American literature, or women's literature at both introductory and specialized levels.

Part I. The "Different" Woman and the Search for a Role

Prose Readings

Emily Dickinson, Selected letters. *The Letters of Emily Dickinson*, ed. T.H. Johnson (Cambridge: Harvard University Press, 1958).
Sylvia Plath, Selected letters. *Letters Home*, ed. Aurelia Schober Plath (New York: Harper and Row, 1975).

Poetry

Emily Dickinson:	"I Think I Was Enchanted"
	"What Soft Cherubic Creatures"
	"Much Madness is Divinest Sense"
Elinor Wylie:	"Preference"
H.D.:	"Helen"
Marianne Moore:	"Tell Me, Tell Me"
Elizabeth Bishop:	"The Moon in the Mirror"
Denise Levertov:	"Melody Grundy"
	"In Mind"
Sylvia Plath:	"Lady Lazarus"
Anne Sexton:	"Her Kind"
	"The Black Art"
Diane Wakoski:	"Movement to Establish My Identity"
Lyn Lifshin:	"Women Like That"

Suggested topics for discussion

> The experience of rejection common to these women
> The scornful treatment of "other" women
> The ideal of beauty and attitudes toward it
> The muse as Medusa, witch-like rather than virginal
> Defiance and self-imposed eccentricity
> A beginning exploration of the form of these poems as it relates to their themes

Part II. Pain and the Paradox of Imprisonment: The Compressive Style

Prose readings

Excerpts from descriptions on women's style in poetry, 1860-1960.
Denise Levertov, "Some Notes on Organic Form," *The Poet in the World* (New York: New Directions, 1973).

Poetry

Emily Dickinson:	"No Rack Can Torture Me"
	"The Soul Selects Her Own Society"
Lizette Reese:	"I Never Talk of Hunger"
Elinor Wylie:	"Let No Charitable Hope"
H.D.:	"I sense my own limit," from *The Walls Do Not Fall*
Marianne Moore:	"Nevertheless"
Elizabeth Bishop:	"Late Air"
Sylvia Plath:	"Mushrooms"
	"Spinster"
Denise Levertov:	"To Speak"
Adrienne Rich:	"A Mark of Resistance"

Suggested topics for discussion

> The nature of the private, inward vision in poetry
> The Imagist influence on women's poetry
> The relation between discipline and liberation in art, technique as discovery
> A working definition of compression in poetry
> The relationship between compression and power; advantages and drawbacks
> The role of the *persona* in the compressive poem

Part III. The Disdain of Sentimentality: "Not Another Poetess"

Prose readings

Theodore Roethke, Description of the "sins" of women poets. *On The Poet and His Craft*, ed. Ralph J. Mills (Spokane: University of Washington, 1965).
Louise Bogan, "Poetesses in the Parlor," *New Yorker* (December 1936).

Poetry

Emily Dickinson:	"After Great Pain a Formal Feeling Comes"
Elinor Wylie:	"This Hand"
H.D.:	"Heat"
	"Oread"
Marianne Moore:	"Silence"
Elizabeth Bishop:	"Sestina"
Denise Levertov:	"The Ache of Marriage"
Sylvia Plath:	"The Applicant"
Adrienne Rich:	"Necessities of Life"
Marge Piercy:	"Sign"
Erica Jong:	"Aging"

Suggested topics for discussion

Implications of the epithet "poetess," for male and female poets

The ways in which feeling is disguised or muted or otherwise denied in these poems

Attitudes toward pain, love, loss—the possibility that the woman in fact perceives and reacts to them differently than the man

The necessity of restraint and irony in order to win critical acceptance

Part IV. The Emerging Female Voice: Regaining Consciousness

Prose Readings

Barbara Segnitz and Carol Rainey, "Introduction" to *Psyche: The Feminine Poetic Consciousness* (New York: Dell Publishing Co., 1973).

Tillie Olsen, "Women Who Are Writers in This Century: One Out of Twelve," *College English*, 34 (October 1972).

Poetry

Emily Dickinson:	"I Started Early—Took my Dog"
	"Title Divine—Is Mine—"
Lizette Reese:	"A Puritan Woman"
Elinor Wylie:	"Little Eclogue"
H.D.:	"At Ithica"
Marianne Moore:	"Marriage"
Elizabeth Bishop:	"O Breath"
Sylvia Plath:	"Daddy"
Denise Levertov:	"Stepping Westward"
	"The Mutes"
Adrienne Rich:	"Translations"
	"From an Old House in America"

Suggested topics for discussion

Means of identifying the "femaleness" of a speaker in a poem
Definition of the literary terms "voice" and "tone"
Means by which the individual experience becomes universal in the poem
Relation between the poet's expression of femaleness and her cultural
context
The "I-Other" relationship with a masculine world
Relation between compressive form and expressive voice
The "touch me/touch me not" aspect of American femaleness and its
relation to poetic form and voice

Part V. The Sense of Kinship Among Women Poets

Prose readings

T.S. Eliot, "Tradition and the Individual Talent," reprinted in *Criticism:
Twenty Major Statements*, ed. Charles Kaplan (San Francisco, Chandler
Publishing Co., no date).
Lucia Getsi, "On Feminine Art," *Illinois Quarterly* (Summer 1975).

Poetry

Elizabeth Bishop:	"Invitation to Miss Marianne Moore"
Denise Levertov:	"September 1961"
Adrienne Rich:	"I Am in Danger—Sir—"
	"The Roofwalker (For Denise)"
Anne Sexton:	"Sylvia's Death"
Carolyn Kizer:	*Pro Femina* (III): "I will speak about women of letters . . . . "
Erica Jong:	"Bitter Pills for the Dark Ladies"

Suggested topics for discussion

Eliot's concept of tradition and how it might apply to women poets
The movement toward "politicization" among women poets and the shift
to an "expansive" form—does it work?
Elements which might be said to comprise a tradition or "memory bank"
for women poets
Reputation of women poets now, and critical reception: what problems
and advantages confront the young woman poet today?
The possibility of a female perception in art related to woman's somatic
and psychological nature

Theory and Resources

One of the problems in designing a classroom exercise is to decide on the approach. The following articles are rich in sources for the study of sexism, including a lengthy resource bibliography for the w.i.l. teacher. Discussion of feminist literary criticism and content analysis, and springboards for specific classroom exercises will be of interest to teachers at all instructional levels.

Celebrating Women

Iris M. Tiedt
University of Santa Clara
Santa Clara, California

*As a means of acquainting elementary students
with various roles played by women, the author has
devised a calendar of the birthdates of famous
women and language activities to be used in
studying these women's lives.*

One of the simplest ways to celebrate the works of women is to observe
their birthdays. Here is a sampling of women to feature AROUND THE
CALENDAR in any classroom.

January

1	Betsy Ross (1752-1836)
5	Christina Rossetti (1830-1894)
6	Joan of Arc (c. 1412-1431)
24	Maria Tallchief (1925-)
26	Mary Mapes Dodge (1831-1905)

February

3	Gertrude Stein (1874-1946)
3	Elizabeth Blackwell (1821-1910)
7	Laura Ingalls Wilder (1867-1957)
9	Amy Lowell (1874-1925)
10	Leontyne Price (1927-)
15	Susan B. Anthony (1820-1906)
17	Marian Anderson (1902-)

March

6	Elizabeth Barrett Browning (1806-1861)
10	Harriet Tubman (1821-1913)
16	Patricia Nixon (1912-)
17	Kate Greenaway (1846-1901)
21	Phyllis McGinley (1905-)
25	Gloria Steinem (1936-)

April

21	Queen Elizabeth II (1926-)
21	Charlotte Bronte (1816-1855)

23 Shirley Temple Black (1928-   )
25 Ella Fitzgerald (1918-   )

May

3 Golda Meir (1898-   )
12 Florence Nightingale (1820-1910)
20 Dolly Madison (1768-1849)
21 Clara Barton (1821-1912)
27 Amelia J. Bloomer (1818-1894)
27 Julia Ward Howe (1819-1910)

June

1 Marilyn Monroe (1926-1962)
7 Gwendolyn Brooks (1917-   )
11 Jeannette Rankin (1880-   )
14 Harriet Beecher Stowe (1811-1896)
14 Margaret Bourke White (1906-   )
16 Katherine Graham (1917-   )
16 Joyce Carol Oates (1938-   )
26 Pearl S. Buck (1892-1973)
27 Helen Keller (1880-1968)

July

6 Della Reese (1932-   )
10 Mary McLeod Bethune (1875-1955)
19 Eve Merriam (1916-   )
22 Rose Kennedy (1890-   )
24 Amelia Earhart (1898-1937)
28 Jacqueline Kennedy Onassis (1929-   )
31 Evonne Goolegong (1951-   )

August

1 Maria Mitchell (1818-1889)
1 Lucy Stone (1818-1893)
12 Katharine Lee Bates (1859-1929)
25 Althea Gibson (1927-   )
31 Maria Montessori (1870-1952)

September

6 Jane Addams (1860-1935)
7 Anna Mary Robertson Moses (1860-1961)
7 Elinor Wylie (1885-1928)
9 Aileen Fisher (1906-   )

14   Margaret Sanger (1883-1966)
14   Kate Millet (1934-   )
19   Rachel Field (1894-1942)
25   Barbara Walters (1931-   )

October

6   Jenny Lind (1820-1889)
10   Helen Hays (1900-   )
11   Eleanor Roosevelt (1884-1962)
14   Lillian Gish (1896-   )
22   Doris Lessing (1919-   )
26   Mahalia Jackson (1911-   )
27   Sylvia Plath (1932-1963)
31   Juliette Low (1860-1927)

November

7   Marie Curie (1867-1934)
12   Elizabeth Cady Stanton (1815-1902)
18   Indira Gandhi (1917-   )
23   Abigail Adams (1744-1818)
25   Carrie Nation (1846-1911)
29   Louisa May Alcott (1832-1888)
30   Shirley Chisholm (1924-   )

December

10   Emily Dickinson (1830-1886)
14   Margaret Chase Smith (1897-   )
16   Jane Austen (1775-1817)
25   Clara Barton (1821-1912)
29   Mary Tyler Moore (1937-   )

Suggested Activities

Suppose, for example, you wanted to celebrate the birthday of SUSAN B. ANTHONY. (Did you know that the California State Education Code, Section 5206, makes this mandatory?) You might begin with a bulletin board display focusing on Ms. Anthony as an individual or you might choose to focus on THE RIGHT TO VOTE.

Present some factual information that is easily obtained in any school encyclopedia. The following is adapted, for example, from the *Encyclopedia Britannica*:

Susan Brownell Anthony was a leader of the women's suffrage movement. Born on February 15, 1820 in Adams, Massachusetts, her work aided the passage of the 19th Amendment in 1920. Cooperating with other early feminists such as Elizabeth Cady Stanton, she fought for the right to vote for women through writing and actively appeared as a voter claiming the right to vote in 1872 which led to her arrest. She died in Rochester, New York, in 1906 before the amendment she sought to initiate was passed.

Talk to members of your classes about planning a celebration on February 15th. Some of the activities they may plan include:

A parade with students dressed appropriately for the late nineteenth century when Susan B. Anthony lived. Make history come alive!

A speaker on the topic of the Women's Movement or contemporary efforts to eliminate sex stereotyping. Consult the local chapter of the National Organization of Women or faculty members of local colleges who may teach Women's Studies courses.

A book display of works by women. Include record album covers and other pictures of women who are active in the equality movement or those who serve as good models of "Women Who Have Achieved."

Student presentations on various ideas presented in contemporary writing related to feminism. They might present a book review of *Born Female* by Caroline Bird or *The First Sex* by Elizabeth G. Davis. Perhaps they would like to review biographies or autobiographies of noted women such as *Blackberry Winter* by Margaret Mead or *Zelda* by Nancy Milford.

A short story by a known woman writer can be featured. Show the film of *The Lottery* by Shirley Jackson or read a short story by Norma Klein, Joanne Greenberg, or Joyce Carol Oates.

These are the kinds of activities that can be developed to celebrate the achievements of any individual woman. Additional sources of information include:

> *Teaching for Liberation* by Iris M. Tiedt. Contemporary Press, Box 1524, San Jose, CA 95109 ($1.50).
> *Who's Who of American Women.* Marquis, annually. (Available in public or college libraries.)
> *Contemporary Authors.* Gale, annually. (Public or college libraries.)

Using Content Analysis to Combat Sexism

Neil Ellman
Hanover Park High School
East Hanover, New Jersey

*The author suggests a method of content analysis
which secondary students can use to recognize
patterns of sexist elements in textbooks and in
the mass media.*

Until nonsexist educational materials are universally available, schools will have to make do with what they now have. However, the easy availability of sexist materials represents a unique opportunity for students to study such materials, and by doing so, to become more sensitive to sexism, even in its most subtle forms.

Most frequently, sexism in textbooks and in the mass media is studied in a very subjective manner. The reader or viewer is able to focus on themes and aspects that are most intriguing, or that most readily coincide with certain preconceptions. It may be easy enough to identify sexist elements in a text, but to note a pattern of such elements is not easy. For this reason, a more objective, quantifiable form of observation is necessary.

No such method is as suitable for the secondary school classroom as is content analysis. In its simplest form, a content analysis consists of a series of specific categories. As one reads a book or views a film, the frequency of occurrences in each category is recorded. The technique has been widely used by social scientists, and now educational researchers, to determine the relative frequency of written and oral occurrences. For example, children's literature has been studied to determine the quantity and nature of violent acts it portrays. What makes content analysis particularly useful in the classroom is the ease with which the method can be handled, even by students inexperienced with other kinds of objective research. Additionally, such research is always original and cannot be copied or paraphrased from reference materials. The process is also one that actively involves students.

The first step in content analysis is the determination of the universe of content to be analyzed. In this case, the universe consists of behaviors, occurrences, language patterns, or characterizations that have reference to gender and sexual orientation.

The second step is the selection of a series of categories that comprise the universe. According to B. Berelson (*Content Analysis in Communication Research*. New York: Free Press, 1952), such categories can be based on words, themes, characters, items, or space-and-time measurements. These categories should be carefully explained to the students, who, aided by the teacher, should decide which category would be most appropriate to the phenomenon they wish to explore.

Words are the simplest forms to categorize. For instance, a student-researcher may choose to read a book and determine how frequently the author uses masculine gender words in reference to males, to females, and to groups that include females. Or the researcher may wish to categorize and quantify the adjectives an author uses to describe men and women.

Themes are more difficult to use, for they are more general in nature. However, the researcher may develop a category system based on such sets of themes as strength and weakness, domination and submission, career orientation and home orientation, etc. Each behavior, occurrence, or utterance that fits one of these categories is recorded. When, for instance, a young girl submits to the will of her brother, the behavior can be categorized as submissive from the girl's standpoint and dominative from the brother's standpoint.

Items are somewhat easier to categorize, for they consist of whole units. An item can be a news article, short story, poem, television program, and so forth. For example, the student-researcher may wish to determine how many television programs have male or female stars; whether female characters are more common in dramas, soap operas, or situation comedies; how many biographies in the school library are of females and males respectively; or how many stories and poems in the language arts anthology are written by males or by females.

Characters are also relatively easy to categorize. How many female and male characters appear in a story? How many female and male scientists are mentioned in a science textbook? How can the female characters in a novel or series of novels be characterized in terms of intelligence, ability, and aspiration?

Finally, *space-and-time* measurements can also be useful. This involves the physical measurement of space and/or time devoted to a theme or character. The student-researcher may determine how many lines of dialogue are spoken by males and by females in a play, or how many column inches of space are given to female reporters in a newspaper as compared to the space given to male reporters.

The students do not begin with a category but with a question to be answered. For example, how much advertising space in a newspaper is devoted to female-oriented products, and how much to male-oriented products? Ideally, the questions should be generated by consultation between the teacher and students. With a less able group or individual, the teacher may present a series of prepared questions. When the research question is properly phrased, it is a relatively easy matter to choose the appropriate category for analysis. The question dealing with advertising calls for a space measurement.

In each case, the student-researcher uses existing and readily available materials to answer the question. It is of critical importance that the students be helped to choose materials that are current and representative. For example, if encyclopedia entries are in question, the latest editions should be used; and if magazines are in question, wide circulation should be a factor in their choice.

If the data generated by such in-class research were an end in itself, little would be accomplished. However, if the data are used to stimulate analysis and discussion, the students benefit tremendously. Having generated original data by experimenting with a simple but effective research device, the students can proceed to explain the data. Why do so few women star in their own television dramatic series? Why are the contributions of female scientists ignored in so many science textbooks? Why do traditional literature anthologies appear to favor male poets and authors? Why are the girls in children's books characterized as submissive and the boys as dominative?

The answers to these questions can be found in a variety of ways. Library research projects are the easiest to implement, but personal interviews, questionnaires, and conjecture are also possible. Indeed, in some instances in which there is a dearth of written material, or in which interviewees are unavailable, a well-argued statement of personal belief may provide the best and only explanation of a set of data. The teacher and student should also be prepared to find no satisfactory answer at all. When, for example, a student asks "Why do traditional literature anthologies appear to favor male poets and authors?" no answer may emerge. The students can interview teachers (themselves literary specialists); do library research; or contact publishers, authors, or writers' associations. Nevertheless, it is a probable outcome of such research that sexism itself—insidious because it has no rational basis—will emerge as the answer. What an awakening for students to realize that some of our most common communication practices are sexist without reason!

The final product of this research can be as varied as the imaginations of the students will permit. Certainly, traditional written and oral presentations will be selected by many students, but the teacher should encourage other presentation styles as well. When no clear answer emerges, or differences of opinion exist in a class, a debate or panel discussion can be structured; when visual materials are used, an exhibition can be arranged; or when music is a subject of analysis, a concert (recorded or live) can be presented. Indeed, the final product can involve more "creativity." If, for example, an encyclopedia entry is discovered to use sexist language, the entry can be rewritten without such language; a sexist song can be rewritten or parodied; or a sexist children's book can be revised. What matters is that the students demonstrate in some way that they can recognize the difference between sexist and nonsexist materials.

Using Literature to Free Students from Homophobia

Gene Stanford
Utica College of Syracuse University
Utica, New York

Specific resources and interesting class activities are used to explore a vital but often overlooked aspect of sex-role stereotyping.

Perhaps the most fundamental reason many people experience anxiety about the changing roles of the sexes is that they perceive any behavior that does not conform to sex role stereotypes as evidence of homosexuality. They encounter a boy who prefers baking bread to playing football and become ill at ease; he's probably "queer" they think. They see a young woman with short-cropped hair, wearing jeans and hiking boots, and titter about her being a "dyke." It really doesn't matter whether the person actually is a homosexual; the important factor is that people fear homosexuality and are nervous about anything, however remote, that might signal its presence. This fear of homosexuality—often called "homophobia"—is, like racism, largely a result of ignorance and mis-perceptions. And it creates misery not only for the person who is genuinely homosexual, but also for heterosexuals who don't fit the narrow defini-tions of male and female that prevail in our society.

Asked to explain their antipathy toward homosexuality, most people point out that homosexuals are mentally ill. They fail to heed the words of

Sigmund Freud, who wrote to an American mother in 1935 that, "Homosexuality is assuredly no advantage but it is nothing to be ashamed of, no vice, no degradation, it cannot be classified as an illness . . . . " In 1973 the American Psychiatric Association struck homosexuality from its official list of mental disorders and issued a statement that "homosexuality in and of itself implies no impairment in judgment, stability, reliability, or vocational capabilities." That action was followed a year later by the American Psychological Association, which in addition to declassifying homosexuality as a "sickness," went on record as "deploring all public and private discrimination against persons who engage in homosexual behavior, in such areas as employment, housing, public accommodation, and licensing."

The official actions of these two groups will probably do little to alter the general public's fear of homosexuality. What is needed is accurate information about homosexuality, and open and enlightened discussion of the topic. Fortunately, homosexuality is the theme of several new books especially suited for adolescent readers, and thus the English teacher can play a significant role in helping students to overcome their homophobia.

The single best book for use in the classroom is *Trying Hard to Hear You* by Sandra Scoppettone (Bantam pbk.). This adolescent novel tells of a teenage girl's discovery that two of her male friends are lovers, and explores the reactions of the other young people to the young men and the girl's struggle to accept the situation. She raises many of the questions any young person has about homosexuality, and the answers she gets (from her mother, a psychiatrist) are accurate and enlightened. The book lends itself particularly well to discussion of the way people mistreat others who are different, and thus it can have impact on students far beyond improving their understanding of homosexuality.

Sticks and Stones by Lynn Hall (Dell pbk.) is another adolescent novel that explores the problems of adolescents rejecting people they don't understand. The main character is not a homosexual, but another boy in his class starts a rumor that he is and the entire community turns against him.

I'll Get There. It Better Be Worth the Trip by John Donovan (Dell pbk.) is a novel most suitable for junior high readers, although some older students may like it. A lonely boy experiments with homosexual behavior briefly and then realizes he wants to grow up "straight." The book implies that an isolated incident does not make one a confirmed homosexual, a concept that is very helpful to many young people.

The Man Without a Face by Isabelle Holland (Bantam pbk.) also tells the story of a young man who has a brief encounter with homosexuality but who does not become a homosexual as a result.

Patience and Sarah by Isabel Miller (Fawcett pbk.) is one of the few books for young readers that deal with female homosexuality. The two women mentioned in the title leave their homes in Connecticut during the 19th century and strike out to homestead in upstate New York. The book explores their attempts to create a relationship for which they have no models or guidelines.

That Certain Summer by Burton Wohl is a novel adapted from the script for a teleplay. It depicts a boy's discovery that his father is a homosexual. The TV drama was heralded as one of the most honest, sympathetic portrayals of homosexuality ever presented on television, and the novel is a fine adaptation. Unfortunately, the Bantam paperback edition is no longer in print.

The Front Runner by Patricia Nell Warren (Bantam pbk.), although not an adolescent novel, is likely to appeal to high school students more than some of the books mentioned previously. It is the story of a college track star, who is openly and proudly gay, and his coach, who becomes his lover.

Any one of these books is an appropriate choice for reading by the entire class, or they can be offered to students as part of an individualized reading program. It is not a mere coincidence that only one of them deals with lesbianism; male homosexuality has always received more attention from writers (as well as psychologists) than female homosexuality. Therefore, the teacher who chooses to use a book that deals with only male homosexuality should take pains to point out to students that the number of female homosexuals in America is approximately equal to that of male homosexuals and should attempt to expose them to information about lesbianism, perhaps through excerpts from a book such as *Sappho Was a Right-On Woman* by Sidney Abbott and Barbara Love (Stein and Day pbk.) or *Lesbian/Woman* by Del Martin and Phyllis Lyon (Bantam pbk.).

More mature readers and teachers who want background information might find the following books of interest:

The Gay World by Martin Hoffman (Bantam pbk.)
Society and the Healthy Homosexual by Dr. George Weinberg (Doubleday Anchor pbk.)
The Gay Mystique by Peter Fisher (Stein and Day pbk.)
Homosexuality Vs. Gay Liberation by Sue March and Walter C. Alvarez (Pyramid pbk.)
The Lord Is My Shepherd and He Knows I'm Gay by Rev. Troy Perry (Bantam pbk.)
Consenting Adult by Laura Z. Hobson (Warner pbk.)
On Being Different by Merle Miller (Popular Library pbk.)
The Best Little Boy in the World by John Reid (G. P. Putnam)
Mrs. Stevens Hears the Mermaids Singing by May Sarton (Norton pbk.)

A "modular learning program" entitled *Homosexuality* is available from Learning Ventures, a multimedia division of Bantam Books. It includes one copy each of the following books: *The Front Runner*, *The Gay World*, *The Man Without a Face*, *Run Softly, Go Fast, Lesbian/Woman*, and *Trying Hard to Hear You*, plus a teacher's guide. If a basic classroom library is desired, this set is quite appropriate.

For the teacher who prefers to approach the topic of homosexuality from the standpoint of literary analysis and criticism, two resources may be useful: *Different: An Anthology of Homosexual Short Stories* edited by Stephen Wright (Bantam pbk.) and the November, 1974 issue of *College English*, a special issue entitled "Homosexual Imagination," available from NCTE.

In addition to reading about gay people, a good way for students to come to an understanding of homosexuality, and thus begin to lose their fear of it, is to interact knowingly with real, live homosexuals. Most university campuses have gay liberation groups who will supply guest speakers; in larger cities the gay organizations have well-coordinated Speakers Bureaus. When arranging for a speaker, suggest that he/she plan to answer questions informally rather than make a formal speech. Prepare the class ahead of time by asking them as a group to draw up a list of questions that they'd like to ask the guest and assign one question to each student to be responsible for asking. For information about the nearest gay organization or speakers bureau, send $1.00 donation for the Gay Activists Alliance's "List of Gay Organizations and Publications" (Box 2, Village Station, New York, New York 10014) or write the National Gay Task Force, Suite 506, 80 Fifth Avenue, New York, New York 10011.

Another useful strategy is to ask the class to remember any jokes about homosexuals they've heard and to recall any TV shows or movies that included homosexual characters. Based on the information they contribute, have them draw up a list on the board of the physical and personality characteristics that jokes and most TV shows and movies assume homosexuals have. Then ask them to contrast these characteristics with the actual characteristics they know homosexuals have from their recent reading or from interacting with homosexuals. Have students come to conclusions about how accurately homosexuals are portrayed in jokes and on TV and in movies.

Examine with the class the types of discrimination in employment and housing and violations of civil rights likely to be encountered by gay people in your community. An excellent resource for this project is *The Rights of Gays* (Avon pbk.).

Show the film "What About McBride?" (CRM Films) which raises the issue of ostracism of a suspected homosexual by his teenaged friends. The film does not resolve the question, but leaves the issue open for students to discuss in class. This would be an excellent film to accompany *Trying Hard to Hear You* and *Sticks and Stones*.

After students have gained new information from reading and other sources, use the following questions for discussion:

a. What do you think causes homosexuality? Have your ideas changed as a result of any reading you've done?
b. Assuming you are heterosexual, how would your life be different if you were gay? What limitations would society put on you? What advantages would you have over heterosexuals? Would you be more happy or less happy than you are now?
c. How would your behavior change if all homosexuals turned green tomorrow? If homosexuals were clearly "visible" in our society, would jokes and ridicule be as likely?
d. How would you respond if you were a parent and discovered your son or daughter was homosexual?
e. Are you aware of any parallels in the problems faced by homosexuals and those of ethnic and racial minorities?
f. How would you react if your best friend confided that he/she was a homosexual?

Have students imagine that they are living in a society in the future in which homosexuals are the majority and only one person in ten is a heterosexual. Laws forbid heterosexuals from engaging in sexual activities with members of the opposite sex, and there is a great social stigma attached to being a heterosexual. Ask: "What changes in your behavior would be necessary under these circumstances? Could you keep your heterosexual identity secret? What would your life be like? Would you try to 'go gay' in order to join the majority because they insist that homosexuality is the only viable lifestyle? Would you 'fight back' against the homosexual majority?"

Another excellent way to introduce students to basic information about homosexuality is the filmstrip program "The Invisible Minority." Winner of the first place award as the Best Filmstrip/Record Educational Program in the National Council of Family Relations competition, this three-filmstrip set is honest and up-to-the-minute. Since it includes interviews with many young homosexuals, it's a good way to introduce students to the fact that most homosexuals are ordinary persons very much like themselves. A teacher's manual suggests follow-up questions for discussion and other activities. This program is an extremely valuable teaching tool, but teachers should certainly preview it before deciding to use it with a class. Available from the Department of Education and Social Concern, Unitarian Universalist Association, 25 Beacon Street, Boston, Massachusetts 02108.

Write the American Library Association Task Force on Gay Liberation (Box 2283, Philadelphia, PA 19103) for a bibliography of books and other materials on homosexuality. They appreciate receiving a stamped, self-addressed envelope. For additional suggestions, see the chapter on "Homosexuality" in *Roles and Relationships* by Gene Stanford and Barbara Stanford (Bantam pbk.), from which much of the material in this article was adapted, and the outline for a mini-course on "Living with Differences" by Gene Stanford and Joanne Bird in *Mini-Guides* (Citation Press pbk.).

English and Feminism, Demands and Rewards

Lallie J. Coy
Triton College
River Grove, Illinois

Lois Josephs Fowler
Carnegie-Mellon University
Pittsburgh, Pennsylvania

The authors explore the ramifications of using feminism as an issue around which to build an English unit or a women's studies course; they mention specific techniques and pieces of literature.

Feminism can serve the teacher and student of English as one of the most potent and effective of focal themes. Like other current social issues, such as ethnic identification or civil disobedience, feminism offers immediacy to attract the indifferent and the awkward. Unlike most such issues, it offers a universality stretching back through time and an immense variety of literature. Besides its attractions it carries added demands and dangers, but the benefits make the costs well worthwhile.

As with other social themes, feminism—which we may define here as a concern, often reformist, with the ways in which females are differentiated from males by society and by nature—provides a broad area of concern, to which a variety of conventional pedagogical matters can be logically related in ways designed to enlist the student's interest. These matters include the study of language patterns, such as denotative and connotative meanings of words, the study of rhetoric, increase in reading skills, such as perception and understanding, and deepening of understanding of differences in patterns of culture.

In dealing with the meanings of words, for example, students might begin by discussing the varied denotative terms for "woman," to such cultural, historical, or regional connotations as "wench," "chick," and "main lady." They might then go on to an examination of these sorts of differences in other languages or in other cultures, to a comparison of differences among dictionary definitions (as between the second and third editions of the Webster's International), and thence to more sophisticated relationships between language and culture.

Feminism, past and present, is a movement that has been steeped in rhetoric of all kinds—from the quiet, more subtle prose of Elizabeth Janeway to the sometimes violent, easily satirized language of Jill Johnston. Analysis of these distinctions for content and for form does increase understanding of the issue and of writing in general. What kind of research clarifies the distinctions between rhetorical devices, rhetorical effectiveness, and judgment of each? Students learn to make informed judgments about what they believe in as it parallels what they hear, read, and see: the difference between hostile, nonfactual writing and that which has a more balanced, even if persuasive, approach; acquiring enough information, past and present, about the roles of women so as not to be misled; assessing accurately, or at least with thoughtfulness, the art of persuasion in regard to substance, content, and reason. Here, too, one can use the feminist issue, not only to help students sort out their own attitudes in thinking and discussion, but also to help them organize attitudes and effects in logical ways so that they, too, can "persuade." Defining an issue, sorting out the implications of one's own relationships with that issue, acquiring more and more information about it, becoming increasingly engrossed in the complexities of it—all contribute to informed judgments, thus a legitimate point of view to write about.

In teaching literature if, as we have suggested, the issue-oriented approach can have potential dangers, it can also have many strengths. Most cognitive research indicates that people learn within a particular context, i.e., they retain and assimilate information that has meaning to them more easily than they do information that is isolated from a conceptual framework. Feminism, as an issue, provides a conceptual framework—one that can be used effectively. If students become interested in the implications of an issue, they tend to read increasingly more difficult material with greater ease. What we suggest here is that in any women's studies course or unit (especially those designed for less agile readers) a sequence be built into the curriculum so that as students become more involved in the issue they can move on to more and more complex material. Few students, unless they are avid readers, will plow through George Gissing's *The Odd Women* or George Eliot's *The Mill on the Floss*. If, however, one begins with Hemingway's "The Short Happy Life of Francis McComber" or even more simplistically with a discussion of "Mary Tyler Moore" or "Maude," then as the contextual framework develops, so will understanding and interest in more difficult material.

Where it is relatively simple to analyze a TV show with students who have watched the program, it is more difficult to motivate discussion and reading of a long, yet relevant work of literature in order to perceive complex interpretations and perceptions of how people act in a particular culture pattern. Working in sequence leads to better understanding and hence motivates reading. If "His Idea of a Mother," a short and easy story by Kay Boyle, inspires a provocative discussion of the psychological complexities of being a mother, that discussion can motivate even reluctant readers to a more eager reading of Doris Lessing's *Summer Before the Dark*. Lessing's controversial psychological study not only inspires fruitful discussion, but also may allow formerly indifferent students to explore similar issues in such traditionally difficult works as *The Ordeal of Richard Feverel* or *The Mill on the Floss*, and earlier works such as Lord Halifax's *Letters to His Daughter*, *Hamlet*, and *Medea*.

The use of feminism as an issue requires that exploration go further than simple reading and discussion of aesthetic literature. Since questions arise that relate to other and parallel disciplines, it is perhaps impossible to teach a course in women's studies that is not in some ways multi-disciplinary. If literature emerges from universal concerns of life, is shaped by a particular culture, and molded by the artist into a verbal form, then a literature-based course in women's studies must consider how culture carries out its modifications.

To look at some of the more popular works now used in such courses, *The Awakening* by Kate Chopin, *Tell Me a Riddle* by Tillie Olsen, *Surfacing* by Margaret Atwood, *Jane Eyre* by Charlotte Bronte, *The Wife of Bath*, and numerous biographies and autobiographies, one cannot discuss them as works of literature alone. In *The Awakening* one should consider roles of women in nineteenth-century America, or the sociali-zation of the idle rich. In *Tell Me A Riddle*, one meets social, economic, and behavioral problems of the aged. *Surfacing* presents the question of parallels between literature and psychoanalytic theory, while *Jane Eyre* offers the rigid processes of socialization of the genteel but poor woman, and *The Wife of Bath* or *Fear of Flying*, the question of definition of the "bawdy" woman. And who would consider working with biography or autobiography outside of historical and social contexts?

The multi-disciplinary concerns of courses focused on a social issue, such as feminism, implies more extensive preparation and a different mode of classroom interaction. Not only do questions involving other disciplines arise, but also questions that touch on personal decisions, values, attitudes, and, most difficult of all, individual relationships. Discussions may be heated; they can rouse conflicts, hostilities, sudden awarenesses, identifications. Defense mechanisms can either stifle or stimulate interaction in ways that differ from the dynamics in a more traditional classroom. Unpredictability is the rule, and it can work for or against a successful teaching-learning experience. Yet if the unpredictable is handled well, the result can be emotionally and intellectually charged in the most positive ways. Flexibility, in an open-ended yet all-encompassing approach to feminism, is one of the most important characteristics needed here by the teacher.

Feminist Literary Criticism: Where to Begin

Carolyn Allen
University of Washington, Seattle
Seattle, Washington

Attention is called to the classroom value of feminist literary criticism now available.

Feminist literary criticism is an area of critical inquiry still in the process of developing a cohesive theoretical foundation, so one of its strengths at the present time is its eclectic empiricism. Rather than a single-minded approach to literature, it is a collection of approaches, growing out of the realization of aware critics, teachers, students, and scholars, that women writers are too often omitted from the accepted literary canon, and that the roles of female characters have been insufficiently discussed. Though some feminist critics see their task primarily as an ideologically prescriptive one, most are concerned with broadening literary discussion not only to include the historical reality of women's relative lack of power, but also to accord women writers the same full, detailed study now given men, and to provide new insights into male texts. They are also pursuing the possibilities of "feminine style" and "feminine consciousness" while continuing to recognize that women writers are as diverse in their individual expression as male authors. They recognize that feminist literary criticism is not intended, even in its eclecticism, to replace more traditional approaches, but to supplement them, to ask new questions, to support its enthusiasms with rigorous scholarship, and to celebrate its commitment to fully integrative and fully human literary discussion.

At the same time as it marks new territory for literary exploration, feminist criticism also challenges the "objective" stance of the critic, and asks readers to recognize that critical values are not free from the biases of the person who imposes them. Teachers of literature as well as teachers of criticism need to be aware of the kinds of questions raised by feminist critics if they and their students are to read literature in a way which records the richness and complexity of female, as well as male, experience.[1]

Following is a necessarily abbreviated summary of the kind of work being done by feminist critics. Although not all have immediate classroom application, together these studies call attention to areas of critical inquiry previously overlooked or insufficiently examined.

A. Reading women writers

1. Serious critical attention to women writers and texts with low visibility in the critical canon or in the college curriculum because the protagonist is female or the style out of the critical mainstream. Examples: Cather, Woolf, Stein, Mansfield, Lessing, Arnow, Stead, Drabble, Atwood. "Serious attention" includes readings which focus on universals such as the dance of death in *Mrs. Dalloway*[2] and obsessive passion in *Nightwood*. Otherwise, women writers and their themes are too easily dismissed as being important only in reference to other women writers or to women readers.

2. Recovery of women writers previously given little or no attention who have literary or cultural importance and deserve to be better

---

[1] There is now a sizable body of criticism which uses, in part or in full, a feminist approach. The teacher wishing to investigate this criticism might best begin with an overview of recent work. Three helpful beginning points of this sort are: Elaine Showalter, "Literary Criticism," *Signs: Journal of Women in Culture and Society* 1 (1975): 435-460; Annette Kolodny, "Some Notes on Defining a 'Feminist Literary Criticism,'" *Critical Inquiry* 2 (1975): 75-92; and Cheri Register, "American Feminist Literary Criticism: A Bibliographical Introduction," in *Feminist Literary Criticism: Explorations in Theory*, ed. Josephine Donovan (Lexington: The University Press of Kentucky, 1975), pp. 1-28. For discussions of feminist criticism in the classroom see *Female Studies*, vols. I-VII.

[2] An interpretation suggested by my colleague, Donna Gerstenberger, with whom I "team-taught" a graduate seminar in feminist criticism.

known. Examples: Elizabeth Stoddard, Charlotte Perkins Gilman, Kate Chopin, Rosamond Lehmann, Marguerite Young.

3. Reevaluation of male criticism on female writers. See, for example, the critical reception of Adrienne Rich, whose books were better received in some reviewing circles before she began to be markedly political and feminist in her poetry. Or see Shoshana Felman's discussion of Balzac's short story, "Adieu" in *Diacritics* (Winter, 1975). The issue is devoted to feminist criticism.

4. Delineation of a "feminine style." Kolodny's article (see note 1) has a useful caveat which cautions against looking for commonalities of style to the exclusion of individual differences. The work in this area still seems tentative, but see Josephine Donovan, "Feminist Style Criticism."[3]

5. Identification and exploration of recurring themes and motifs in literature by women. See, for example, the psycho-mythological work of Annis Pratt, especially her forthcoming book on fictional motifs. See also Sydney Kaplan's discussion of feminist consciousness in her *Feminine Consciousness in the Modern British Novel.*[4]

6. New uses of traditional genres. Examples: Isak Dinesen's shifting of gothic conventions in *Seven Gothic Tales* or Margaret Atwood's reassessment of mythic values in the "Circe/Mud" poems of *You Are Happy.*

7. Greater recognition of other forms of literary creativity, particularly of autobiography where women have done much work.

B. Reading male writers

1. Examination of images of women in literature, including such stereotypes as Earth Mother and Bitch/Goddess. As Showalter points out (see note 1), this kind of criticism has, through replication, lost its ability to provide much new insight, but it is still useful in the classroom as a means of showing how women characters are repeatedly cast in prefabricated molds. Identification of the stereotypes leads to more interesting questions about why these characters appear formulated as they do in literature; at that point, literary criticism becomes intimately tied to social, cultural, and economic history, and to psychology.

2. Readings of standard texts insufficiently noted by traditional criticism. Examples: the degree to which Olive Chancellor dominates *The Bostonians* even though Basil Ransom is the ostensible hero;

---

[3] In *Images of Women in Fiction: Feminist Perspectives,* ed. Susan Koppelman Cornillon (Bowling Green: Bowling Green University Popular Press, 1972), pp. 341-354.

[4] Urbana: University of Illinois Press, 1975.

Caddy as the central figure in *The Sound and the Fury* even though she is not given a section to narrate.

3. Analysis of the ways in which some male writers portray women as objects over whom men exert their power, sexual and otherwise. The most powerful example is still Kate Millett on Henry Miller and Norman Mailer, in *Sexual Politics*,[5] but repeated negative attacks, even for a politically illuminating purpose, are finally not very useful as a critical tool. Showalter calls this sort of criticism "beating a dead pig" (p. 452). For the insights Millett provided one male critic, however, see James Miller, Jr., "The Creation of Women: Confessions of a Shaken Liberal."[6]

Feminist critics generally agree about the need for a variety of approaches to literary texts. Debate continues, however, about the goals for the whole enterprise. Prescriptive critics, such as Millett, argue that feminist literary criticism is finally cultural criticism,[7] and they see their analysis as a tool for better understanding how women have been culturally and politically oppressed. Theirs is criticism in the service of wide-ranging political analysis. Others concentrate their efforts on the literature itself in order to assert the rightful place of women writers in literary history; they recognize that their work may well mean reassessing that history as it now stands. Neither group, though, would disagree with Rich's hope for a criticism which "would take the work first of all as a clue to how we live . . . and [to] how we can begin to see—and therefore live— afresh."[8]

Rich's hope for a new kind of criticism carries with it not only a sense of engagement, but also of subjectivity. Feminist criticism recognizes that the "objective" critical norm of the "detached" critic is neither objective nor detached nor inclusive. Meanings, as David Bleich has pointed out, are constructs, not discoveries,[9] and critics make constructs as they read texts— constructs based on their own intellectual and cultural biases and on their own experience. What books they analyze, what focus they give, what mode they use to express their convictions all are matters of personal choice. The subjectivity of the feminist critic does not mean lack of rigor, or lack of attention to the text, or vague impressionistic rambling. And

---

[5] New York: Doubleday, 1970.

[6] *Centennial Review* (Fall, 1975).

[7] Register, p. 10.

[8] "When We Dead Awaken: Writing as Re-Vision," in *Adrienne Rich's Poetry*, ed. Barbara Charlesworth Gelpi and Albert Gelpi (New York: W.W. Norton, 1975), p. 90.

[9] "Pedagogical Directions in Subjective Criticism," *College English* 37 (1976), p. 457.

though it may grow from a political sense that too much of women's experience has been missing from literary discussion for too long, it does not mean vision narrowly restricted by ideology. Rather, subjectivity in criticism and in the classroom connects an intellectual and emotional life with professional work, and encourages students to do the same.

A Basic Resource Bibliography for the Teacher of Women in Literature

Susan Waugh Allen
Meramec Community College
St. Louis, Missouri

The theme of this year's publication makes a resource bibliography an appropriate and valuable inclusion even though it is not a classroom practice.

The special focus on literature by and/or about women and its incorporation into college courses are such recent developments that most teachers are struggling with their own self-educations while they try to teach their classes. I hope this list of resources will help teachers of Women in Literature to keep up with the explosion of materials in the field during the next few years. It is meant as a "bibliography of bibliographies," and attempts to list *where good current materials are likely to be found during the next few years.* You will probably notice its rather schizophrenic nature, often listing a major "source of sources" such as *Womenhood Media* in one section, and a single source of rental films in another. When I list an obscure single source, it is because it has not appeared in a larger bibliography, though *this* list is far from exhaustive. I have tried to divide the list into useful sections, and hope it will help you find and keep up with the growing number of resources for the teacher of Women in Literature.

Ideally, the teacher of Women in Literature should become acquainted with the basic resources, get on mailing lists, work with the library, and update sources and materials periodically. As a starting point, you might want to give a copy of this bibliography to your library's reference department.

Basic Sources

Ahlum, Carol, and Fralley, Jacqueline M. *A Guide to Curricular Materials*. Old Westbury, New York: The Clearinghouse on Women's Studies (Box 334, 11568).

$1.00 plus 25¢ postage. An excellent guide which covers several disciplines.

THE CATALOGUE available from: Women's Studies Research Center, 2325 Oak Street, Berkeley, California 94708.

THE CATALOGUE is sold for $16.00 complete; you may order for much smaller amounts the sub-sections, which include such valuable items as: Bibliographies on Women, Indexed by Topic; Directory of Women's Periodicals; NOW Newsletter Directory; List of Gay Women's Periodicals; Female Artists Past and Present. Send for price list.

The Feminist Press, SUNY/College at Old Westbury, Box 334, Old Westbury, New York 11568.

Write for the free catalogue, another adventure in things we all need. The Feminist Press carries many of its own original books, including: Feminist Resources for Schools and Colleges; Who's Who and Where in Women's Studies; Nonsexist Materials for Elementary Schools; Strong Women: An Annotated Bibliography; High School Feminist Studies; Women's Studies for Teachers and Administrators: A Packet of Inservice Education Materials. The Feminist Press continues KNOW's *Female Studies* series, including *Guide to Female Studies* (nos. I-III), and *Female Studies* (nos. VI-X).

Grinsted, Kirsten, and Rennie, Susan, eds. *The New Woman's Survival Catalogue*. New York: Coward, McCann & Geoghegan (Berkley Publishing Co.), 1973. (To be revised and updated.)

This enormous red paperback (published by the company that brought out *The Whole Earth Catalogue*) is A MUST. It contains information about every conceivable subject related to women. The section beginning on page 135 is of special interest to us, and you will find only a few of the TNWSC listings here. There are lists of scholarly library collections all annotated, and lists of women's studies centers all over the country. Also contained herein are extensive lists of women's organizations, newspapers, magazines and book presses. You will be pleased at their variety and number.

KNOW, Inc., P.O. Box 86031, Pittsburgh, Pennsylvania 15221.

Write for KNOW's catalogue, and begin benefiting from an important source. Among KNOW's publications are several which every teacher of women in literature should read: *Female Studies I-V*. All these booklets are by distinguished teachers of women's studies; some contain practical advice on organizing and teaching w.i.l. and other women's studies courses; some approach literature from a feminist perspective. *Women's Work and Women's Studies*, 1971 and 1972 (will be continuing). Contain *excellent* bibliographies! Send for current catalogue and price lists.

Robinson, Lora H. *Women's Studies: Courses and Programs for Higher Education.* ERIC Higher Education Report no. 1, 1973.

Describes women's studies programs all over the country; it is essential for those setting up new courses and programs. Send $3.00 to: American Association for Higher Education, One DuPont Circle, Suite 780, Washington, D.C. 20036.

University of Michigan computer index to Women's Studies; write to: Ms. Nancy Grosso, Women's Studies Department, University of Michigan, Ann Arbor, Michigan 48104.

This promises to be our most promising single resource. Beginning in the fall, 1975, the computer will be fed a steady and rich diet of Women's Studies resources. The printouts will be made available at reprint cost (minimal) and will be constantly updated. The Women's Studies Department, through a grant, is conducting this fine project.

Wheeler, Helen. *Womanhood Media: Current Resources About Women.* Metuchen, N.J.: The Scarecrow Press, Inc., 1972.

A MUST. If you and your library do not have this book, order it at once. It provides access to books, periodicals, organizations, AV resources, and even out-of-print titles. It also contains a "basic book collection" on women for libraries, and numerous treasures for the researcher and teacher. The book has excellent methods of access to all kinds of materials. Many sources that might have been in this document are thoroughly collected in *Womanhood Media.*

The Woman's Center, Barnard College, New York, New York 10027.

The Woman's Center publishes *Women's Work and Women's Studies,* a valuable and *ongoing* source containing good literary bibliography, including criticism and dissertation abstracts. A MUST. The Woman's Center at Barnard collates current research on women and publishes the results. Keep up with its activities.

Bibliographies

A Gay Bibliography.

Annotated lists of source materials of all kinds, available from: Task Force on Gay Liberation, American Library Association, Box 2383, Philadelphia, PA 19103.

Arora, Ved Parkash, compiler. *Women: A Selected Bibliography.* Regina, Saskatchewan: The Provincial Library.

This active library has published a number of bibliographies; send for more information.

Austin, Helen S.; Suniewick, Nancy; and Dweck, Susan. *Women: A Bibliography on Their Educations and Careers.* Washington, D.C.: Human Services Press, 1971.

Excellent annotated bibliography with full abstracts. Good "Beyond the Findings" essay at the beginning. Contains much research relevant to w.i.l. teachers and their students. A MUST.

Business and Professional Women's Foundation, 2012 Mass. Ave., N.W., Washington, D.C.

Publishes several bibliographies, including one for working women.

Chamj, Betty E. *American Women and American Studies*. Women's Free Press.

Includes bibliography.

Cisler, Lucinda. "Selected Bibliography on Women." In *Rebirth of Feminism*, edited by Judith Hole and Ellen Levine. New York: Quadrangle/The New York Times Co.

Short annotated bibliography.

Cisler, Lucinda. *Women: A Bibliography*.

Annotated and extensive, covering several fields, available from: Lucinda Cisler, P.O. Box 240, Planetarium Station, New York, New York 10024. 50¢ prepaid.

Cornillon, Susan Koppelman, ed. *Image of Women in Fiction Perspectives*. Bowling Green: Bowling Green University Press, 1972.

Contains five collections of essays and an excellent annotated bibliography.

Davis, Lenwood G., compiler. *Black Women in the Cities: 1872-1972*. Council of Planning Librarians Exchange Bibliography, no. 336, 1972.

Fries, Maureen. *Ongoing Bibliography*.

Bibliography of writings by and about British and American women writers. Fredonia, New York: Department of English, SUNY, 14063.

Gage, Nancy, ed. "Bibliography of Bibliographies." In *Women's Rights Almanac*. Elizabeth Cady Stanton Publishing Co., 1974.

Excellent list, annotated; pp. 591-595.

Jacobs, Sue Ellen. *Women in Perspective: A Guide for Cross Cultural Studies*. Urbana, Ill.: University of Illinois Press, 1974.

Especially useful for anthropology, this book would help us in foreign language and other areas. Part I covers the world by continent and country; Part II is indexed by subjects such as education, sex, history, etc.

Kirchmar, Albert. *The Women's Rights Movement in the United States, 1848-1970: A Bibliography and Sourcebook*. Metuchen, N.J.: Scarecrow Press, 1972.

Kuda, Marie J., ed. *Women Loving Women*. Chicago: Lavender Press (Box 60206, Chicago, Illinois 60660), 1974. $1.50.

Selected annotated bibliography on the lesbian in literature.

Library of Congress, Washington, D.C. 20540.

Obviously a good general source; will send a list of its publications; has excellent selective bibliographies and reading lists on women.

Manley, Seon, and Belcher, Susan. "O those extraordinary women, or the joys of literary lib." Radnor, Pa.: Chilton Book Co., 1972.

Contains short bibliography.

Murray, Michele. *A House of Good Proportions: Images of Women in Literature.* New York: Simon and Schuster, 1973.

A fine anthology with an excellent introduction, this book contains an unannotated but useful list of women poets and of words in all genres about women. It is my favorite bibliography for students' use.

Neglected American Women Writers.

Send for publication with bibliography to: Priscilla Allen, 444 N. Park, Bloomington, Indiana 47401.

Nower, Joyce, compiler. *Bibliography of Women Writers.* San Diego, Calif. (866 24th Street, 92101). 50¢.

PMLA (Publication of the Modern Language Association).

A comprehensive bibliography of the year's work in all the language areas comes out annually. Unfortunately, articles relevant to w.i.l. are not indexed; many hours must be spent sifting.

Westervelt, Esther M. *Women's Higher and Continuing Education: An Annotated Bibliography with Selected References on Related Aspects of Women's Lives.* New York: CEEB, 1971.

Write: Educational Testing Service, Princeton, New Jersey. Excellent abstracts, many in educational research, and many in literature.

Williams, O. "Bibliography of Works Written by American Black Women." *College Language Association Journal* 15 (1972): 354-77.

Women and Literature: An Annotated Bibliography of Women Writers. 1973.

Excellent reference list, available from: The Sense and Sensibility Collective, 57 Ellery Street, Cambridge, Mass. 02138. $1.50. This fine, thorough bibliography is indispensable. The Collective's fine work is continuing and well worth a periodic inquiry.

Women's History Research Center, Inc., 2325 Oak Street, Berkeley, California 04708.

One of the most important libraries for women in literature, history, etc., in the country, the center publishes *many* bibliographies. Write for a price list.

Women—To, By, Of, For and About. Box 3488, Ridgeway Station, Stanford, Conn. 06905.

Woodworth, Anne, compiler. *Women: A Guide to Bibliographies.* Toronto Reference Department, reference series #15. Toronto, Ontario: John P. Robarts Research Library, University of Toronto. $1.00

Books

A flood of women in literature books, most of good quality, has begun to pour into our offices from the commercial publishers, and can be easily located through *Books in Print* and *Paperback Books in Print*. *Womanhood Media* and *The New Women's Survival Catalogue* offer more feminist and unconventional sources for books than the usual places do. The listings in TNWSC, especially, are a treasure trove, and contain descriptions of the important library and research collections. Some other "finds" follow; addicted bibliophiles will delight that *Book Review Index* can now be supplemented with more exotic fare.

American Library Association, American University Press Service, Inc., One Park Avenue, New York, New York 10016.

Has lists of university press books for and about women.

"The American Woman: As Seen Through the Eyes and Pens of 19th and Early 20th Century American Women Novelists and Poets." Oliver Oriole Booksellers, 412 South Benton Way, Los Angeles, California 90057.

This bookstore specializes in first editions. The catalogue is a delight in itself; send for it for the illustrations alone.

Argosy Book Stores, Inc., 116 East 59th Street, New York, New York 10011.

Send particularly for catalogue #613: "Women: Biographies of Notable Women Throughout History."

Burt, Franklin, Lenox Hill Publishing and Distributing Company, 235 East 44th Street, New York, New York 10017.

Send for catalogue #178, "Women and Feminism."

"A Catalogue of Old, Used, Rare and Out-of-Print Books on Women and Feminism " available from: Q.M. Danbrey and Company, Box 31061, Washington, D.C. 20031.

Feminist Book Mart, 162–11 9th Avenue, Whitestone, New York 11357.

Good source—send for catalogue.

Gerritsen Collection of Women's History (1543-1945), University of Kansas. Microfilm available fall, 1975 from: Microfilming Corporation of America, 21 Harristown Road, Glen Rock, N.J. 07452.

An excellent very new source.

Microfilming Corporation of America, A New York Times Book Company, 21 Harristown Road, Glen Rock, N.J. 07452.

Microfilming enormously increases our access to out-of-print or obscure works that are rediscovered. Catalogues are published periodically.

"Periodicals on Women's Rights." Greenwood Press, 51 Riverside Avenue, Westport, Conn. 06880.

A new research collection in microfilm.

"Women: Parts I & II: A Catalogue of Over 700 Facsimile Reprints." Books for Libraries, 1 DuPont Circle, Plainview, New York 11803.

The Women's Guide to Books.

A periodic annotated catalogue of books sold directly by mail; published three times a year. Order first issue for $2.00 (prepaid): MSS. Information Corporation, 655 Madison Avenue, New York, New York 10021.

University Microfilms: A Xerox Company, 300 North Zeeb Road, Ann Arbor, Michigan 48106.

This is especially good for reprints of out-of-print books; send for "Women in Contemporary Society: A Catalogue of Dissertations."

Films and Media

Establishment films are being produced in this area now, but *Womanhood Media* and *The New Women's Survival Catalogue* provide good access to media materials, many of which are useful supplements to w.i.l. classes. The following will help, too:

Betancourt, Jeanne. *Women in Focus.* Pflaum, 1974, bibliographical index. LC 74-78728.

The *most complete* catalogue of films about women. This book contains synopses and suggests books to be read in conjunction with the films.

Media Report to Women. 3306 Ross Place, N.W., Washington, D.C. 20008. Dr. Donna Allen, editor and publisher.

This service tries to keep up both with print and media sources of interest to women in communications, and with women themselves. Send $6.00 for the annotated *Index/Directory*, $10.00 for a year's microfilm of the service.

The Women's Movement: A Multimedia Guide, Bowker, ISBN 0-8352-0711-0. Soon to be published.

This promises to be a valuable resource.

Periodicals

Both *Womanhood Media* and *The New Woman's Survival Catalogue* contain detailed lists of feminist and other relevant periodicals, so I need not repeat them here. Here are the scholarly journals and some other good sources that you will not find in WM or TNWSC. Indexes which are selecting women's materials will include: *The Essay and General Litera-ture Index, Public Affairs Information Service, Katz Magazine for Li-braries* and *The New York Times Book Review Index.*

Aphra, Box 355, Springtown, Pa. 18001.

Well-known feminist literary journal.

Feminist Studies, Ann Calderwood, editor. 417 Riverside Drive, New York, New York 10025.

Interdisciplinary scholarly journal.

"Herstory," Micro Photo Division, Old Mansfield Road, Wooster, Ohio 44691.

An excellent women's periodical collection.

International Journal of Women's Studies, Barbette Blackington, editor. Interna-tional Center for Women's Studies, Washington, D.C.

Excellent international, interdisciplinary scholarly journal.

Library Journal.

Excellent articles on resources for women, many especially relevant to the w.i.l. teacher.

Media Report to Women, 3306 Ross Place, N.W., Washington, D.C. 20008.

For $10.00 a year, a constant update on the *Index/Directory* on women's sources and women in communications.

Ms.

Frequently publishes excellent articles about women writers, past and present, as well as poetry and other relevant articles.

Publisher's Weekly.

A good source for w.i.l. teachers; a good way to find out what's going on in the book world.

Signs: Journal of Women in Culture and Society, The University of Chicago Press, 11030 Langley Avenue, Chicago, Illinois 60628.

A quarterly publication (1 year, $12.00) containing a variety of facts and ideas from many fields, including English, history, economics, health, and psy-chology. Scholarly, diverse, and analytical.

Women and Literature, Janet M. Todd, editor. Department of English, Douglass College, Rutgers University, New Brunswick, N.J. 08903. $7.00.

A semi-annual devoted to women writers and women as characters prior to 1900. In the fall, a bibliography is published.

Women's Studies Abstracts, P.O. Box 1, Rush, New York 14543. Sara Stauffer Whaley, editor.

A quarterly publication which abstracts feminist and "establishment" periodicals, this is a very valuable resource! The list of periodicals abstracted is itself an excellent list of the major feminist and other relevant periodicals.

Women's Studies: An Interdisciplinary Journal, Wendy Martin, editor. Gordon and Breach Science Publishers, Inc., 440 Park Avenue South, New York, New York 10016.

This is good reading, and the interdisciplinary approach is helpful.

Women's Studies Newsletter, published quarterly by the Feminist Press, Box 344, Old Westbury, Long Island, New York.

A good continuing resource. The Feminist Press is to be praised.

Other periodicals which already contain some useful articles include: *College Composition and Communication, College English, PMLA, Research in the Teaching of English, Abstracts of English Studies, American Literature.*

Organizations

Clearinghouse on Women's Studies, The Feminist Press, Box 334, Old Westbury, New York. In addition to its press activities and *The Women's Studies Newsletter,* the Feminist Press's "Clearinghouse" keeps track of women's studies courses and who teaches them (publishing *Who's Who and Where in Women's Studies*).

Conference on College Composition and Communication, Women's Exchange, c/o Julia Haggar, Des Moines Area Community College, Ankeny, Iowa 50021.

MLA, Commission on the Status of Women, Elaine Reuben, Bascom Hall, University of Wisconsin, Madison, Wisconsin 53706.

Excellent source for information about women in the profession and other relevant matters. Look up "Affirmative Action for Women in 1971: A Report of the MLA Commission on the Status of Women in the Profession," *PMLA,* May, 1972.

The Woman's Caucus of the Modern Language Association. WORK IN PROGRESS c/o Delores Barracano Schmidt, English Department, Slippery Rock State College, Slippery Rock, Pa. 16057.

Keep up with the caucus's activities.

National Organization for Women (NOW). National office: National Press Building, Washington, D.C. 20004.

Founded in 1966, this organization's activities include some publishing, usually on political and social issues. Local chapters of NOW also have a variety of materials, and it's worth keeping up with NOW for many reasons. Send for "By and About Women" from NOW, 45 Newbury Street, Boston, Mass. 02116.

National Council of Teachers of English, 1111 Kenyon Road, Urbana, Ill. 61801.

An excellent source of publications to help us in every phase of our teaching, NCTE publishes a free catalog called *Resources for English and the Language Arts*. You can also receive *free*: #19859, "Guidelines for Publications" (helps determine whether or not a publication deals fairly with women), and #19557, "Guidelines for Confronting Attitudes that Penalize Women." If you are not familiar with the following, please send for: *A Case For Equity: Women in English Departments*, Susan McAllester, ed.; "Women Writing and Teaching," Elaine Hedges, guest editor, *College English*, Oct. 1972. Essays in this issue, including a moving piece by Tillie Olson, are excellent and essential for the w.i.l. teacher. A MUST.

National Council of Teachers of English, Committee on Women, c/o Lallie J. Coy, English Department, Triton College, 2000 Fifth Ave., River Grove, Ill. 60171.

WEAL (Women's Equity Action League), Education and Legal Defense Fund, 795 National Press, Washington, D.C. 20004.

In addition to its other important activities, publishes relevant booklets such as "Women and Fellowship," by Judith Nies, which, for $1.00, gives information on fellowships available to women. Write for other publications.

Women's Caucuses and Committees in Professional Organizations available from: AAUW (American Association of University Women), 2401 Virginia Avenue N.W., Washington, D.C. 20037.

The AAUW itself publishes a fine set of materials. Send for Ruth Oltman's *Campus 1970: Where Do Women Stand? Research Report of a Survey on Women in Academe*; ask for AAUW's catalogue.

Women's Organizations and Leaders (annual), Myra E. Barner, ed., Today Publications and News Service, Inc., National Press Building, Washington, D.C. 20004.

Some Good Anthologies: 1975-1976

Autobiography

Goulianos, Joan, ed. *By a Woman Writt: Literature From Six Centuries By and About Literature*. Penguin. $2.45.

Excellent collection with a lot of variety, from the obscure to Mary Shelley and Mary Wollstonecraft. Does not emphasize the modern, and has a difficult reading level, so may not be suitable for all classes. Includes the first extant autobiography in English written by a woman.

Merriam, Eve, ed. *Growing Up Female In America: Ten Lives*. Dell. $1.50.

Something here for everyone, with all kinds of variety. This book is a natural for an interdisciplinary course focusing on American women in history and literature.

Drama

Sullivan, Victoria, and Hatch, James, eds. *Plays By and About Women*. Vintage Grove. $2.25.

Very good collection of twentieth century plays with a variety of female characters.

Fiction (Short Stories)

Cade, Toni, ed. *The Black Woman: An Anthology*. Mentor. $1.25.

Also contains some essays and poetry, with a variety of authors and themes.

Ferguson, Mary Ann, ed. *Images of Women in Literature*. Houghton Mifflin. $4.95.

Excellent introduction preceeds stories divided into groups according to the types of women characters depicted therein: the dominating wife, the old maid, etc. A fine collection.

Murray, Michele, ed. *A House of Good Proportion: Images of Women in Literature*. Simon & Schuster. $3.95.

My personal favorite, this collection begins with a moving introduction by the editor, who recently died of cancer at the age of forty. Murray divides the stories into groups slightly different from Ferguson's, based partly on stages beginning with the Little Girl. This book contains an excellent bibliography/reading list that my w.i.l. students love.

Sargent, Pamela, ed. *Women of Wonder: Science Fiction Stories by Women About Women*. Vintage Grove. $1.95.

Schneiderman, Beth Kline, ed. *By and About Women: An Anthology of Short Fiction*. Harcourt Brace Jovanovich. $4.95.

Fine collection by modern writers, also divided; very good reading.

Poetry

Bernikow, Louise, ed. *The World Split Open: Four Centuries of Women Poets in England and America, 1552-1950*. Vintage. $3.95.

This excellent book contains a preface by Muriel Rukeyser and a fine introduction. It covers so many poets that it may not have your favorites by them, but I'm glad it's here—especially for the early poetry, so little of which is in print.

Chester, Laura, and Barba, Sharon, eds. *Rising Tides: Twentieth Century Women Poets*. Pocket Books. $1.95.

Good small samplings with photographs and short biographies preceding, with some rather obscure poets included.

Howe, Florence, and Bass, Ellen, eds. *No More Masks!* Anchor. $3.95.

Excellent anthology with good introduction and solid selections of a large number of poets, including the best known.

Segnitz, Barbara, and Rainey, Carol, eds. *Psyche: The Feminine Poetic Consciousness*. Dell. $1.50.

> Does many of the same things as *No More Masks!*, but not as thoroughly. Good contemporary collection.

Also of Interest

Cornillon, Susan Koppelman, ed. *Images of Women in Fiction: Feminist Perspectives*. Bowling Green University Press, 1974.

> Contains a good sampling of writing about women in literature and an excellent bibliography.

Showalter, Elaine, ed. *Women's Liberation and Literature*. Harcourt Brace Jovanovich, 1974.

> Contains an abundance of materials of all stripes for good discussions of issues surrounding women in literature and women writers.

Female Studies IV (from KNOW).

> Contains a long annotated bibliography of anthologies, although it is now somewhat out of date.

There are an increasing number of non-fiction books such as *Up From The Pedestal* and *Voices From Women's Liberation* that might work well in interdisciplinary courses.